2-16-89

For dearest Elliot —
A belated ♡ Day to
the best dressed guy
alive! We're positive
this book will all be
review for you, but
just in case...

Lots of love —
Libby
&
Rick

A GENTLEMAN'S WARDROBE

Harmony Books
New York

A GENTLEMA

N'S WARDROBE

*C*lassic *C*lothes
and the *M*odern *M*an

by

*P*aul *K*eers

CONTENTS

*F*OREWORD

There are certain classic clothes which have a place in history, but a timeless appeal. Created in the past, they are still worn in the present. They have the look, the construction, and the tradition, which makes them absolutely *right*. These are the clothes in A Gentleman's Wardrobe.

Behind most items in a gentleman's wardrobe there lies a story. Classic men's clothes were not born from a designer's drawing board, or from the seasonal whim of a couturier. They have come down to us on the backs of practical men, whether sportsmen or soldiers, wealthy or working men. Classic menswear is not about designer names; it commemorates, among others, the Duke of Wellington, the Prince of Wales, Lord Raglan, the Earl of Cardigan, the Duke of Norfolk and the Earl of Chesterfield. Its history is as much about common sense as dress sense.

It's a history which explains not only what men wear, but the way it should be worn: why the bottom waistcoat button is always left undone; why some overcoats have black velvet collars; why brogues have holes and why lapels have notches. And perhaps it also explains why most classic menswear has remained unchanged for over fifty years, and much for a century or more. Like great-grandfather, like son.

The classic wardrobe is largely a product of what fashion historians call the Great Masculine Renunciation, when the Industrial Revolutionaries gave up the lace and brocade of the dandy, and established the sober, serious dress of the Victorian gentleman. It was a wardrobe which asserted the power, status and formality of the English –

and it established the idea echoed by F. Scott Fitzgerald, that 'Gentlemen's clothes are a symbol of the "power that man must hold, and that passes from race to race"'.

Once the Duke of Windsor had performed his personal transformation of the rules, the classic wardrobe was firmly established. As the French designer Yves St Laurent has pointed out, 'By 1930 to 1936, a handful of basic shapes were created that still prevail today as a sort of scale of expression, with which every man can project his own personality and style.'

Because they were worn by the most senior Englishmen, these clothes had to be the best. Quality materials and traditional craftsmanship combined to create items that were both flattering and functional, hard-wearing and well made. And they were also expensive – the only things top tailors don't cut are corners.

As gentlemen's dress became the uniform of the new, white-collar workers, cheaper versions began to filter into the menswear market. And gradually the old principles and the time-consuming details were ignored, by a generation of office workers with their synthetic suits and drip-dry shirts – by men with higher standing, but lower standards.

But classic clothes and accessories are still available today. They are investments, items whose look will last as long as their superior quality. They are still being worn and used by the senior English men.

The details incorporated by those original tailors have remained, as the hallmark of items which are still constructed with the same care and attention. Those details have become the sign of a gentleman who cares about his wardrobe. Once you're aware of the details, they can never be ignored. 'Once you know about it, you start seeing it,' said the writer and social observer Tom Wolfe. 'There are just two classes of men in the world. Men with suits whose buttons are just sewn on to the sleeve, just some kind of cheaper decoration, or – yes! – men who can unbutton the sleeve at the wrists, because they have real buttonholes and the sleeve really buttons up.'

Traditional manufacturers have retained all these classic details. They are a symbol of a determination to uphold the standards of the past, the outward sign of a concern that also extends to the cloth and the construction. And the likelihood is that a manufacturer who ignores traditional details, who puts convertible cuffs on a buttondown shirt, or notched lapels on a double-breasted jacket, will have equally scant regard for the traditions of quality construction.

In the absence of seasonal fashions, these kinds of styling details signal a man's sartorial awareness. Only such tiny, distinguishing elements are permitted in the uniform of power and status. They reflect a man's income and his sense of tradition. And they show, in a discreet but emphatic way, whether he really understands the principles of classic menswear.

Of course, a gentleman can get by without understanding his wardrobe. He can also eat steak with a fish knife, or drink claret from a champagne flute. It would be terribly unfair to judge him by any of these things. But as Oscar Wilde once said, 'Only a fool would *not* judge by appearances.'

'A gentleman will take care that his clothes are of the best quality, well-made and suitable to his rank and position.'

PRINCE ALBERT

PART I
Basics

'The sense of being perfectly well-
dressed gives a feeling of inward
tranquility which religion is
powerless to bestow.'

RALPH WALDO EMERSON

*T*IES

It was in the 1950s that Lord Tonypandy first entered Parliament as George Thomas MP, a young and inexperienced member for South Wales. He began his career determined to make a good impression in a new suit and tie, and so he was horrified when, as he entered the House, the Tory benches burst into uproar. A furious Conservative chief whip rose hurriedly, beckoned him into the centre of the chamber and, to a background of shouts and cries, whispered urgently, 'Are you aware that you are wearing an Old Etonian tie?'

'No,' replied Thomas in all honesty. 'I bought it in the Co-op in Tonypandy!'

The future Speaker of the House of Commons had not yet learnt the language of the most eloquent item in a man's wardrobe.

It was around 1670 when a separate neck-cloth began to be worn in place of spreading lace collars, but the term 'necktie' was not used until after about 1830, when cravats began to be worn wound once around the neck and then tied in front with a large bow or knot. It was the 'four-in-hand' knot, with two long, trailing ends (like the reins of a coach and four) which developed into the tie as we know it today.

Then, in the nineteenth century, there was an enormous expansion of both English public schools and the sports they played. Sporting colours proliferated, in order to distinguish not only the different schools, but also different teams and houses within the schools. The supporters wore their team's colours in striped bands around their boaters. But then someone had the bright idea of taking off his hat band and tying it around his neck. The old school tie was born.

As the tie took over from the cravat in popularity, so the fashion for coloured stripes spread across the ties of schools, clubs, and regiments (which took their colours from the distinctive facings on their traditional uniforms). Not all organisations adopted stripes; the London Scottish RFC is one of the oldest crested club ties, while the tie of the famous Leander Club is a plain but unmistakable pink (known properly as cerise). The brighter team colours, intended to edge a cricket sweater or show up through the mud of a match, were never meant to be worn with a business suit, so some of the louder stripes have now been replaced, for everyday purposes, with more wearable designs. But behind many of the original colours lie suitably colourful stories.

The tie of the Royal Military Academy, for example, bears colours which represent the ingredients of gunpowder – yellow for sulphur, blue for saltpetre and black for carbon. The Royal Tank Corps takes its stripes from the brown mud, red blood and green fields of Flanders. And the famous dark blue and magenta Guards tie is said to represent the blue blood of the Royal Family with the red blood of the Brigade.

P. L. Sells & Co., the largest tie manufacturers in England, have over 10,500 patterns on file to be made up when required. Even allowing for their enormous variety of colours and combinations, there are inevitably some clashes: a member of the 2nd/4th Grenadiers (Indian) could be confused with an Old Boy of Westminster Hospital, while an Old Woodruffe could pass for a member of the Cambridge University Ski Club. Indeed, one Old Harrovian never wore his famous tie

Some schools have two ties; the country pattern is bolder.

A knitted tie suggests a creative spirit.

The rules say silk for the City, wool for weekends.

The old school tie can be worn anywhere.

The star of the stripes – Eton's true blues.

Sporting stripes and formal crests – the ultimate school combination.

In town, discreet symbols (hippopotami) replace Leander Club's traditional pink.

The most popular business tie – still spotted everywhere.

Bolder stripes play on a sporting tie like the Harlequins'.

again, after someone once asked him, 'Which years were *you* at Monkton Combe?'

The finest ties in the world are still woven from English silk reppe; Sells get theirs from an East Anglian mill run by direct descendants of the Huguenots. The colours sing out of silk reppe because the weft is floated on the surface of the material instead of being woven in. On the reverse, such ties are always darker, because all the coloured threads are on the front of the material. And the stripes on an English tie commonly run from the left shoulder down towards the

A silk tie should always be properly untied, and not simply slipped off without undoing the knot. Hung up overnight, the creases will then fall out. In particularly bad cases put the ends of the tie together and roll it up like a belt, smoothing out the creases as you go. Leave it rolled for one night, then hang it up, and it should return to its original state.

There are still many traditional English establishments, from the dining room at the Ritz to the pavilion at Lord's, where ties *must* be worn. But should they be old school ties? Bamber Gascoigne, himself an Old Etonian,

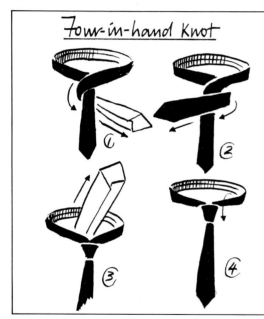

The four-in-hand knot makes politician Norman St John Stevas appear straightforward – unlike his tie.

right; on an American tie they run from the right shoulder to the left, because manufacturers in the US cut the cloth face down.

Fine ties are cut on the bias, which helps them knot properly and stops them twisting round against the shirt. To test whether a tie is cut on the bias, hold it up by its smaller end, and see whether it twists round or hangs straight. If it twists, reject it.

was once walking through the officers' mess at Chelsea Barracks with a friend who was wearing his OE tie, when a crusty character in an armchair lowered his newspaper, and glowered at the pair. 'I understood,' he declared, 'that one never wore one's Old Etonian tie in town.'

'As a matter of fact, sir,' replied the young chap smartly, 'I'm just going to the country.'

'Well, I understood,' continued the voice, 'that if one was going to the country, one changed into one's Old Etonian tie at the Chiswick roundabout.'

One colonel insists that you only wear a Brigade tie at the annual wreath-laying in the Guards Chapel and at the garden party, and in any case *never* after six p.m. Yet Michael Heseltine put one on for almost every speech as Minister of Defence, presumably to present an air of military authority. (He was indeed in the Welsh Guards – for his National Service.)

The most significant ties remain those of the great English networks – the stripes of the top public schools and the Oxbridge colleges, the magenta and blue of the Guards and the 'rhubarb and custard' of the MCC. Ironically, many Old Boys regard with suspicion anyone who feels the need to advertise membership of their network by wearing their tie. But if one sin is greater than wearing no tie at all, it is wearing a tie to which one is not entitled. For like any signs of status, old school ties can only be worn by those who have genuinely earnt their stripes.

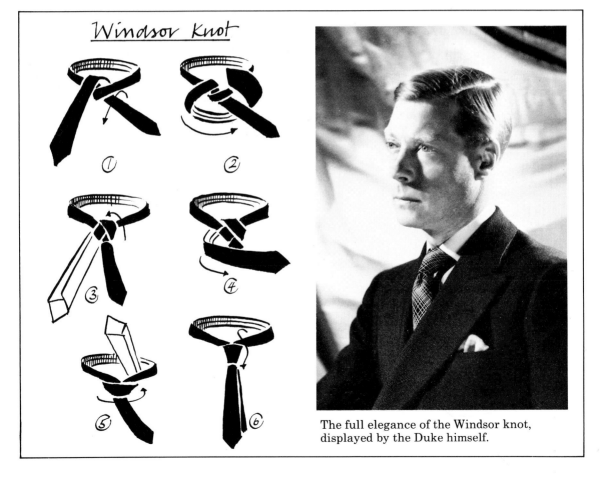

The full elegance of the Windsor knot, displayed by the Duke himself.

THE BOW-TIE

Bow-tie

The modern bow-tie is a direct descendant of the basic
eighteenth-century stock; now, its ends are shaped into bats'
wings (straight) or thistles (curved). Who wears them today?
Men like Arthur Schlesinger, who says 'They are a great
convenience. It is impossible to spill soup on a bow tie. In fact,
it requires extreme agility to spill anything on it at all.'

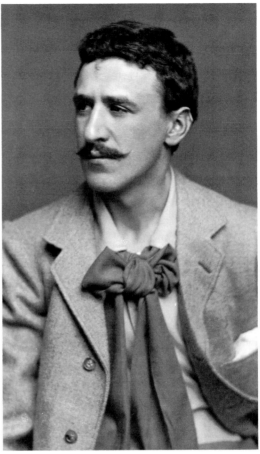

Oscar Wilde himself shows how the modern style of neckwear is tied to the past, with a bulky example of the transition from cravat to tie in 1891. The knot, a yachting knot known in France as a *régate*, was tied in the same way as today's basic four-in-hand. Meanwhile in 1893, the designer Charles Rennie Mackintosh wears an original four-in-hand necktie, its trailing ends reminiscent of a horse's reins. This artistic style was the forerunner of the present-day bow-tie.

Shirts

When the Great Gatsby threw open his wardrobe, it revealed shirts 'piled like bricks in stacks a dozen high'. All, of course, were bought in England: 'shirts of sheer linen and thick silk and fine flannel ... shirts with stripes and scrolls and plaids in coral and apple-green and lavender and faint orange, with monograms of Indian blue.'

They made Daisy cry, because she had 'never seen such beautiful shirts before'. But shirts with coral scrolls or apple-green plaids hardly fall into the classic. In fact, at the turn of the century one commentator stated quite categorically that 'the striped, coloured or pique collar almost invariably bespeaks the bounder'.

The white shirt has always been the symbol of the gentleman. Because it soils so easily it became an indication of a man who, if he worked at all, worked at a desk (a 'white-collar worker'), and a man who could afford a good laundry. A collar and cuffs 'which bore the ineffaceable signs of cheap laundering', wrote Arnold Bennett, 'reflected the shadow of impending disaster'. Few men, however, went as far to avoid this as Julius Beerbohm, who sent his shirts from London to Paris every week to be washed.

Even striped shirts had a rough passage into the gentleman's wardrobe. In the 1870s, when they were introduced, they were known as 'regatta shirts', and were not considered suitable for business wear, particularly if the object was to disguise the day's dirt. 'Figures and stripes do not conceal impurity,' warned an etiquette book in 1876, 'nor should this be a desideratum in any decent man.' The path to acceptance lay in attaching white collars and cuffs, the signs of a gentleman, to striped and coloured shirts – a style that survives in the City.

CONSTRUCTION

The first shirts pulled directly over the head; it was as late as 1871 when Brown, Davis & Co. of Aldermanbury registered the first design in England in the 'coat style', which opens all the way down the front. Today, this is available in either plain or placket front. The placket, once a strip of additional material, is now a stitched fold of the shirt-front fabric itself, which gives additional strength to the join of the shirt.

A fine shirt will be held together with single-needle stitching. This means that the seams are stitched with one needle, first down one side of the seam, and then down the other. The cheaper method is to sew with double needles, which is faster, but can lead to puckering after washing.

Two other indications of a carefully made shirt are the pleats at the point where the sleeve joins the cuff – the more pleats the more complex the construction and the more elegant the cut – and the gauntlet button, which lies on the sleeve of a quality shirt and closes the gap at the wrist. Once it was used to roll back the cuffs while washing; now it's simply a sign of added attention to style.

Equally, a vertical seam on the shoulder yoke of a regular shirt hints at craftsmanship. This is an echo of the split yoke used by bespoke shirtmakers at the back of a made-to-measure shirt, in order to adjust the height of each shoulder separately. Given that some cheap shirts now do away with a shoulder yoke altogether, a split yoke is a sign of extra concern for tradition.

How to fold a shirt

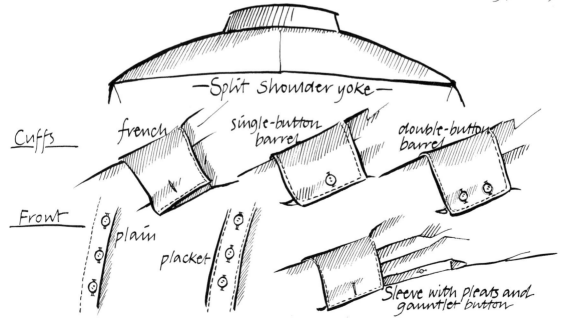

Button shirt and lay face down — Fold one side across — Fold first sleeve down

Fold second sleeve across — Fold second sleeve down — Fold shirt at waist — Ready for storage

—Split shoulder yoke—

Cuffs

french

single-button barrel

double-button barrel

Front

plain

placket

Sleeve with pleats and gauntlet button

Any colour you like, so long as it's white – any fabric you like, so long as it's linen. The Victorian gentleman didn't look for variety in his shirts, even if they were tailor-made. They were completed with cufflinks, placket buttons and stiff, upright collars; H. G. Wells's character Kipps forced himself into fashionable versions 3 in high, which 'made his neck quite sore and left a red mark under his ears'.

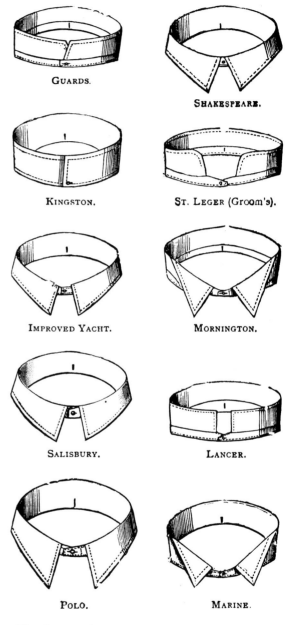

GUARDS.

SHAKESPEARE.

KINGSTON.

ST. LEGER (Groom's).

IMPROVED YACHT.

MORNINGTON.

SALISBURY.

LANCER.

POLO.

MARINE.

The downturn of the collar meant an upturn in variety – a range of styles from 1884.

A traditional shirt does not have a breast pocket. These were only added following the demise of waistcoats, and a gentleman would certainly not put anything into one even if it were provided. But a traditional shirt does have a generous tail, cut up over the thighs and curved at the base. Once, in order to keep the shirt in place, its tail could actually be buttoned to the front between the legs. Although this proved rather awkward, the fact that the tail and front can meet is still a clear indication that a shirt has a comfortable length.

COLLARS

There is an American claim that they – and specifically Mrs Orlando Montague of Troy, New York – invented the detachable collar. In 1827 Mrs Montague, realising that the body of her husband's shirts rarely needed washing as often as the collars, cut the collars off, and sewed on strings to reattach them after washing. The Rev. Ebenezer Brown, realising the commercial possibilities, began selling the new detachable collars in his store. And soon gentlemen were condemned to struggle, first with strings and then with studs, to keep their shirt on.

To save money on cloth collars, Victorian gentlemen wore paper, celluloid, and even patent waterproof collars, which H. G. Wells described as 'one of those you wash overnight with a toothbrush and hang on the back of your chair to dry, and there you have it, next morning, rejuvenesced'. There was an astonishing variety, with upright styles particularly popular, of which only the wing collar on dress shirts survives. By the turn of the century the modern turndown collar had come into vogue, coinciding with the demise of the cravat, and in the 1930s the arrival of the Van Heusen collar, with fabric woven on the curve for a better fit and the

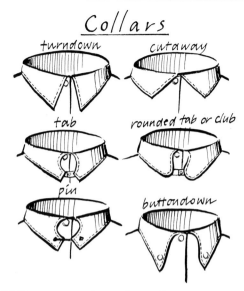

Collars
turndown   cutaway
tab   rounded tab or club
pin   buttondown

fold line woven into the collar, was greeted with sighs of relief.

Some say the separate collar was killed off by the open-necked shirts of the 1960s while others blame the regulation shirts with attached collars of the Second World War. But to compensate, styles in turndown collars have proliferated.

The most formal remains the broad turndown. The length of the points has fluctuated with tie widths – the longest were known as Barrymores, after the actor John Barrymore who favoured them – but they have now settled at between $2\frac{5}{8}$ in and $2\frac{7}{8}$ in. A fine turndown collar will always have a line of stitching around the edge, omitted from cheaper versions.

The cutaway was designed to accommodate the broad Windsor knot. Smaller, modern ties with four-in-hand knots may look a little lost in its broad spread, but it remains the favourite collar style of Prince Charles.

The tab collar was first worn by the Duke of Windsor on a visit to the USA, where it

Cottoning on to the new City etiquette; you can go long on gold, but you must never go short on shirtsleeves.

was so enthusiastically adopted that it is now thought of as an Ivy League style. (In fact, Ivy Leaguers prefer the rounded tab or club collar popularised by Eton schoolboys.) The tab, which pulls the collar wings together, was originally held by a brass stud; modern versions use a press fastener, but some Jermyn Street shirtmakers still produce a model which is held by a button. It is still primarily an American collar style, regarded warily by more formal Englishmen.

The pin collar draws the wings of the collar together and raises the tie in a rather more formal manner. Collar pins have a removable end, replaced after the pin has been pushed through the collar wings, although some modern designs simply grip the two collar wings without piercing the material. The result is dressy, but a trifle flash.

The buttondown collar, derived from the polo shirt, is considered on p. 25.

All collars are fitted to a neck measurement taken just below the Adam's apple. It's worth remembering that Cary Grant failed his first screen test because at 17 in, he was told, his neck was too thick.

CUFFS
The cuffs of a shirt have always protruded beyond the cuffs of a jacket. The style originated when men had lace ruffs to display, and a show of white has been seen ever since. Half an inch is expected to be revealed nowadays.

Cufflinks should only be worn with the formal, folded-back French cuff. This cuff, which cannot be buttoned, should only be combined with formal collar styles such as turndown, cutaway or pin. Casual collar styles are usually paired with the two-button barrel cuff. The only universal cuff is the single-button barrel, which can be matched with any collar. The so-called convertible cuff is a barrel cuff which can be worn with either buttons or links, but this is a confused and ugly modern aberration.

CLOTH
A crisp cotton poplin, which breathes with the body and holds dyes well, is the premier shirting. Poplin is a plain weave cotton, with as many as 144 warp ends to the inch. The best is of two-fold staple yarn, that is, of two single yarns twisted together. And the best 'superfine' cotton is Sea Island cotton, because of the staple length. In American cotton each individual fibre has a length of about 1 in; in Egyptian cotton $1\frac{1}{2}$ in; and in Sea Island cotton, grown in the soil and climate of the Caribbean, the fibres are 2 in long, producing a superior cloth.

If poplin is perfect for the City, Oxford cotton is ideal for less formal shirts such as the buttondown and tab collar. This is a

The Polo Shirt

At the turn of the century the rules demanded that tennis was played in long-sleeved dress shirts. One singles champion in particular objected to the rules – René Lacoste, a player so fast that the French nicknamed him *Le Crocodile*. He set about inventing his own, short-sleeved, tennis shirt. It was made from a resilient cotton piqué knit, and it was based on the long-sleeved polo shirt (itself a successor to the buttondown shirt originally worn by polo players). A crocodile sewn on to the breast identified an original René Lacoste shirt.

In 1929 Lacoste became a professional shirtmaker; his design became known as a polo shirt, and it has been widely copied, although a crocodile symbol still identifies a genuine Lacoste. But its success lies in the fact that it is not only worn for competition; the comfortable cotton piqué shirt with a polo collar has been sported as casual wear, by such distinguished men as J. F. Kennedy.

softer cotton, comfortable and hard-wearing; after a lengthy battering the only sign of wear tends to be small balls of material which are rubbed up inside the neck. This, known as 'pilling', can be removed simply by running an electric razor around the collar.

Outside town, only one fabric is suitable for the countryside. This was invented in 1890 by Henry Ernest Hollins, a Derbyshire mill owner who was told that it was imposs- ible to combine the warmth and durability of wool with the weight and comfort of cotton. Viyella, his brand of union cloth, a blend of 55 per cent merino wool with 45 per cent long- staple cotton, named after the Via Gella on which his mill stood, is the result of his determination. Its flannel-like nap can take patterns like tartan without running, and in a Tattersall check (named after the patterned horse blankets used in Richard Tattersall's famous market), it is made up into the classic country shirt.

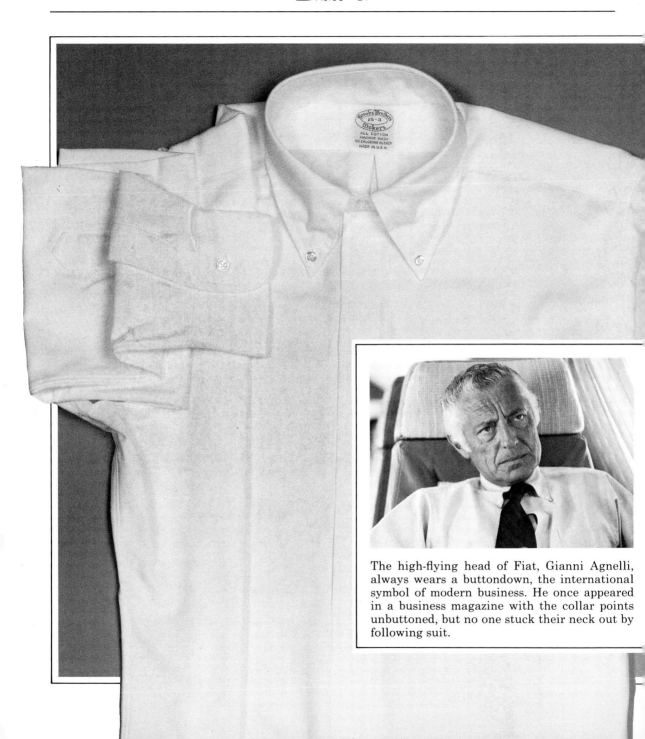

The high-flying head of Fiat, Gianni Agnelli, always wears a buttondown, the international symbol of modern business. He once appeared in a business magazine with the collar points unbuttoned, but no one stuck their neck out by following suit.

THE BUTTONDOWN SHIRT

A spectator at a turn-of-the-century English polo match would have noticed that the wealthy players wore formal cotton dress shirts – but with the collars buttoned down so that they didn't flap about during the match. One such spectator was John Brooks, president of Brooks Brothers store on Madison Avenue. Brooks took the idea home to New York, and so in 1900 the buttondown shirt was born.

There is now a fifty-step tailoring process involved in manufacturing the classic Brooks Brothers buttondown. In eighty-seven years only two changes have been made to the shirt: originally it was a pullover shirt, but this has been replaced by the coat style; and in the 1960s, in response to the demise of the waistcoat, a breast pocket was added. But the essential buttondown, with its comfortable rolled collar and Oxford cotton ideal for long daily wear, has remained the same. Popularised by American businessmen, it has become the hallmark of the international executive – so much so that when Mary McCarthy published a story called *The Man in the Brooks Brothers Shirt* everyone knew what she meant.

SUITS

The Savile Row suit has come to epitomise the finest outfit that a man can own. Its quality and construction are designed to last ten years; the details, which continue to denote a classic suit, have lasted even longer. As one firm of English tailors expressed it, 'If you can keep your suit when all around are changing theirs, then you are a man, my son.'

BESPOKE TAILORING

Since bodies cannot be acquired off the peg, fine suits are unlikely to be acquired in a similar manner. Bespoke tailoring got its name because the clothes were literally 'bespoken' – spoken for or ordered – by the customer. And some Savile Row customers still refuse to wear the tailor's prestigious label inside the jacket, because it's *their* suit; the tailor merely put it together.

The bespoke tailoring of Savile Row has reigned supreme ever since the world's oldest surviving tailors, Poole's of Savile Row, received their first warrant of royal appointment from Emperor Napoleon III. Today, Savile Row's fame has spread so far that from a mispronunciation of the famous street name the Japanese for a suit is 'sabiro'.

In Victorian times the tailors would take a dozen fittings to perfect a suit, but this was actually a sign of incompetence rather than of care. Savile Row cannot afford such hit and miss methods today; modern materials can't be manipulated like the old heavyweight suitings, and modern executives don't have that kind of time to spare. So the standard of cutting has had to improve. A Savile Row suit today will require an average of three fittings; the tailoring takes less time, but actually requires more skill.

A minimum of twenty measurements are taken for the coat, which is how the tailors still refer to the jacket. (If the sleeves are too long, the customer is said to be 'overcoated'.) The terms used to discuss the customer's figure are in an efficient (and discreet) code; DRS, for example, is a Dropped Right Shoulder; FS is a Forward Stomach; and BL1, 2 or 3 are Bow Legs to the First, Second or Third degree. The trousers themselves require a minimum of five further measurements. It then takes twice as long to cut the initial paper patterns from these measurements as to execute the cutting of the pieces which make up the suit itself. The templates are kept, and updated on every visit; a top tailor has around 9,000 in store.

The subsequent 'try-ons' guide the tailor towards a precise fit. The customer is asked to put wallet, keys and other accessories into the appropriate pockets, to ensure that they are allowed for in the finished garment. Final adjustments are marked on the cloth with traditional tailor's chalk. The entire garment is sewn by hand, except where the tailor chooses to use his own, personal machine; the buttonholes alone on a Savile Row suit take four hours work. And the result will fit as only the finest bespoke suit can: on Savile Row the only thing which fits like a glove *is* a glove.

Because the Savile Row suit is 'bespoken',

the tailors will never state which details ought to be incorporated. They will advise a customer, but, as one tailor expressed it, 'Only the arrogant would say they dictated.' So for details, the customer must take guidance from tradition. The only other, more general advice is the way in which tailor Cyril Langley, of Albemarle Street, complimented the taste of one of his celebrated clients, the poet T. S. Eliot. 'Remarkable man, Mr Eliot,' he commented to another customer. 'Nothing ever quite in excess.'

CUT

It was the cut of the suits which the Duke of Windsor wore on his international visits that ensured Savile Row's modern status. They were cut somewhere between the comfortable but shapeless sack suits of the United States, and the square-shouldered, sharply waisted jackets of the European tailors. The Savile Row suit of the 1930s struck an ideal balance: shoulders which were naturally shaped with only slight padding, a definite waist, but a soft construction and a comfortable way of moving. And popularised by the Duke, together with smart dressers like Fred Astaire, this is the basic cut which has now lasted for over fifty years.

The most popular suit on Savile Row today has a single-breasted, two-button, vented jacket, gently shaped, with a firm but not padded shoulder line. (The trousers have straight legs and plain bottoms, and are held up with a belt.) It is a natural development from the suit cut by the same businesses

So far, sew good – the first fitting of a bespoke suit.

between the wars; it is still comfortably unrestricting, yet flatteringly elegant.

Even royalty accept the importance of the way a suit hangs on a man. Admiral Sir John Fisher once appeared before King Edward VII, wearing a decidedly elderly outfit. 'That is a very old suit you are wearing,' the King remarked. 'Yes, sir,' he replied. 'But you've always told me that nothing really matters but the cut.'

Two- or three-piece
The original matching suit consisted of three pieces – coat, vest and breeches – as dictated by Charles II when he invented the waistcoat (p. 34). This was the suit which established English tailoring across European society. The waistcoat never recovered from the cloth restrictions of the Second World War, and the heating in modern offices has rendered it virtually redundant. But as off-the-peg suits have become almost universally two-piece, so a matching waistcoat has now become a way of signifying a bespoke suit.

Single- or double-breasted
By the time the suit had developed into its modern form, both single- and double-breasted fastenings were common. Both are equally acceptable on an English suit, providing that the detailing is correct. However, the double-breasted jacket must always be buttoned when standing, and should not be worn with a waistcoat.

Whether single- or double-breasted, a man's jacket always buttons left side over right. This originated in order to avoid catching the pommel of one's sword in the opening, when drawing it right-handed.

Lapels
Jacket lapels are derived from the high-collared tunics of military uniform. To make

Singularly elegant – T. S. Eliot's single-breasted, three-piece suit is a business cut and a business colour: 'Dark, dark, dark.'

themselves more comfortable, soldiers unfastened the upper buttons, and rolled back each side. When the fashion spread into civilian clothes, tailors retained the notch (indicating the break of the original collar) and the buttonhole (where the tunic would have fastened at the neck). The width of these 'notched' lapels has fluctuated in conjunction with collars and ties, but a classic lapel extends to a fraction less than half-way across the chest of the jacket.

In addition to notched lapels there are 'peaked' lapels. With the exception of dinner jackets (p. 112) these should only be worn

Doubly immaculate – Richard Nixon's double-breasted, two-piece suit is precisely cut, the first of many things he kept close to his chest.

on double-breasted jackets, where there is traditionally a buttonhole on each lapel. Notched lapels should only be worn on single-breasted jackets, *never* on double-breasted ones.

VENTS

The vents in the rear of the jacket came from riding wear: they were originally designed to allow a jacket to part over the back of the horse behind the rider. This freedom of movement (and of access to trouser pockets) survives in both single- and double-vented jackets.

Double-vented jackets, the traditional English style, move more easily, and allow the best access to pockets. They also emphasise the line of the body, making them particularly elegant on a tall, slender figure, but they will draw attention to wide hips or a prominent rear.

Single-vented jackets, favoured by Americans, smooth over the line of the body, and allow access to trouser pockets with the penalty of dividing at the rear, and making the figure appear slightly shorter. A single vent was also stylistically correct with a three-button jacket.

Non-vented jackets, popular with European tailors, hang with perfection, but bunch up as soon as the wearer puts his hands into his trousers, or sits down.

If vents are worn, they should be short enough (7 to 9 in) to function without calling attention to their presence.

POCKETS

The traditional English suit jacket has two flap pockets, one on either hip. The fashion for a third, smaller ticket pocket is now restricted to sports jackets. Jetted or besom pockets have spread in popularity; they are normally sold stitched closed, and as there are no flaps to disguise sagging of the opening in use it is acceptable to leave them sealed for neatness and never use the pockets.

In either case, the welt pocket is the only acceptable style of breast pocket. It is a mark of good tailoring that the suit pattern continues without a break over pocket welts and flaps.

Patch pockets are the most casual in style, and should only be worn on single-breasted country suits. They are better worn on sports jackets, to which pleated and bellows pockets are restricted. These pockets were

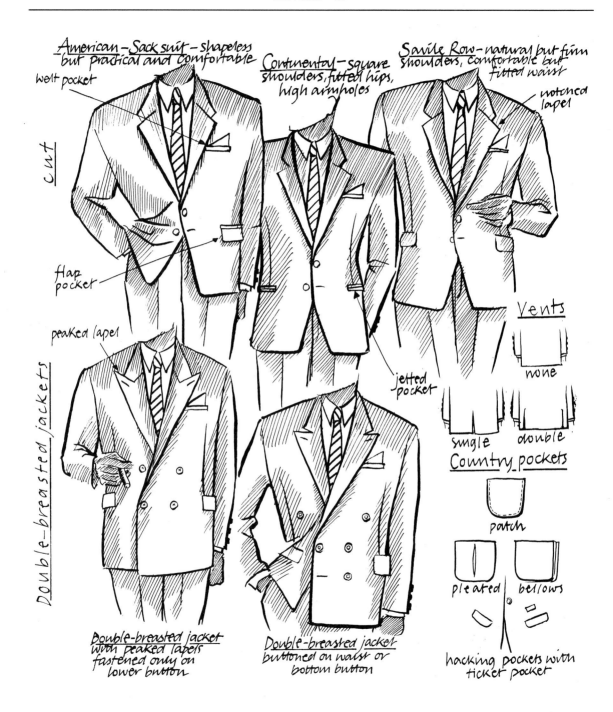

American – Sack suit – shapeless but practical and comfortable

Continental – square shoulders, fitted hips, high armholes

Savile Row – natural but firm shoulders, comfortable but fitted waist

welt pocket

notched lapel

cut

flap pocket

peaked lapel

jetted pocket

Double-breasted jackets

Double-breasted jacket with peaked lapels fastened only on lower button

Double-breasted jacket buttoned on waist or bottom button

Vents

single   double

Country pockets

patch

pleated   bellows

hacking pockets with ticker pocket

designed to swell with the additional depth of gun cartridges, and should not be worn on suits. Equally, the angled flap pockets known as hacking pockets are so-called because they are designed for easy access while horse-riding; they, too, should be reserved for country jackets.

FRONT BUTTONS

The single-breasted jacket has gradually reduced its buttons, from three at the turn of the century to a brief vogue of one in the 1960s. Three-button jackets are still worn today, and old-established tailors still argue that this is the 'correct' style. But Savile Row has settled on two, and only the upper of those two should ever be buttoned, as the jacket is balanced to close at that point. The lower button should never be fastened, either on its own or with the upper button.

Many double-breasted jackets are now cut in such a way that they can *only* be fastened on the *lower* button. This was a style introduced by the Duke of Kent, when he wore a double-breasted jacket with long rolled lapels and the waist button undone, giving a longer line to the jacket. This elegant look was then copied by tailors, who cut the front so that the waist button could not actually be fastened. If a double-breasted jacket does provide the option of fastening either button, it is proper to leave either one undone.

SLEEVE BUTTONS

Napoleon first put buttons on to the cuffs of his soldiers' uniform, to stop them wiping their noses on their sleeves. The buttons on the cuffs of suit jackets were put there to enable the sleeves to be rolled back while working. But off-the-peg suits could not have working buttons, because then the sleeve could not be altered (except by unpicking the armhole). So one of the hallmarks of a

bespoke suit has always been that it has working cuff buttons.

Richard Sennett, in his book *The Fall of Public Man*, explains the English situation perfectly. 'One could always recognise gentlemanly dress because the buttons on the sleeves of a gentleman's coat actually buttoned and unbuttoned,' he said, 'while one recognised gentlemanly behaviour in his keeping the buttons scrupulously fastened, so that his sleeves never called attention to this fact.'

MATERIAL

In classical literature the words 'wool' and 'clothing' were often synonymous. In classic tailoring the same is also true. Wool is hard-wearing, resilient, and 'breathes' with the body, unlike any artificial fibres.

Suiting is classed by its weight; before the Second World War a winter suit could be made up from 20 oz cloth, but now the heaviest material, which combines warmth with hard wear, is around 16 oz. A fine, tropical suiting can be as light as 8 oz. A tailor will always ask about the purpose of a suit, and the temperature in which it will be worn, before suggesting a weight between those extremes. For a business suit he is likely to suggest a woollen worsted. Some material, like gabardine, is difficult to tailor elegantly, while the harsh finish of fabrics like mohair and tonic create a stiff, unnatural cut. The ideal is a worsted, which is soft, strong, drapes elegantly and wears well.

COLOURS

Any serious suit is dark in colour, and has been for centuries. When the Napoleonic court was all glitter and gold, Beau Brummell put the Prince of Wales into black and dark blue, and high society in London dressed almost entirely in black. As Britain

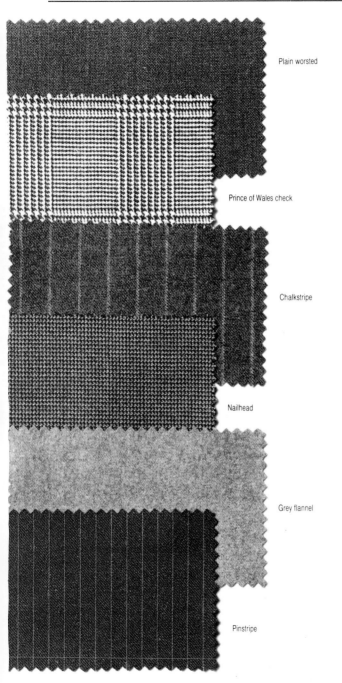

Plain worsted

Prince of Wales check

Chalkstripe

Nailhead

Grey flannel

Pinstripe

emerged victorious, so the capitals of Europe followed suit, into the colours of Protestant modesty, and there men have remained. 'Nowadays,' wrote André Gide, 'if men are more serious than women, it's because their clothes are darker.'

Blue is simply the most suitable colour for business wear. Charles Revson, head of the Revlon empire, had suit fittings three times a week, and over a period of twenty years amassed a collection of more than 200 suits – almost all of them dark blue. The classic City businessman has always worn a dark blue pinstripe and the uniform has become universally respected.

Black is the most formal of suit colours, closest to the frock coat that was the accepted business wear in the City well into this century. A black suit now is very much as Browning described one, 'courtly once and conscientious still'.

Grey became popular as a business suiting in the 1950s, and the title of Sloan Wilson's novel, *The Man in the Grey Flannel Suit*, summed up the way that the colour dominated corporate culture in the United States. It has now been adopted in the City, especially by those who take their lead from the faster, more aggressive business style of the USA.

Brown should only be considered as a country colour. In fact, several City firms have told their employees that they consider brown suits to be 'unprofessional'. This is nothing new; when Julius Beerbohm received a visit from his brother wearing a reddish-brown suit, he turned his face to the wall and said disgustedly, 'Ginger!' Charles Revson went further: he said simply, 'Brown looks like shit.'

PATTERNS

Younger designers produce suits in attract-

The Victorians were not really in a position to suit themselves. The frock coat, with its distinctive straight front edges, had not appeared until after 1815, but by the end of the century it was the hallmark of respectability. Here, in 1870, the bearded Charles Dickens is a picture of Victorian professional formality, in a short, double-breasted frock coat, with waistcoat, light-coloured trousers and top hat. When the matching lounge suit first arrived it was worn only on informal occasions; Benjamin Disraeli is seen wearing a single-breasted version with a soft, informal hat. But by the late 1890s, an observer at Charing Cross noted that lounge suits out-numbered frock coats by three to one, and gradually they became accepted as formal business wear.

ive checks, herringbones, birdseyes (the small, dotted fabrics also known as 'nailhead') and many other regular and irregular patterns. Yet there are only three patterns which remain as classic as the suit itself.

Pinstripes are thought to derive from the ledger lines in books of accounts. This, and the link with the old 'Stock Exchange rig' of striped trousers with a black frock coat, has established the pinstripe as the traditional City suiting.

Chalkstripes owe their enormous success to the world tour undertaken by the Duke of Windsor in double-breasted, chalkstripe suits. The popularity of these wider stripes with gamblers and racketeers is thought by some to have given birth to the phrase 'wide boys'.

Prince of Wales check is the popular name for what is actually a fine coloured overcheck on a Glen Urquhart plaid. Many of the Victorian gentry who bought Scottish estates were not entitled to a clan tartan, and so created 'district checks', to be worn by ghillies, stalkers and estate employees. Glen Urquhart plaid was the estate check of the Countess of Seafield.

AGE
No suit should look new. Anderson & Sheppard of Savile Row believe that if a customer leaves their shop and is recognised as wearing a new suit, then they have failed to do their job. Beau Brummel had his valet wear all his new clothes first, to take the vulgar newness out of them. The modern suggestion is that having a suit cleaned removes the dressing in the cloth and takes away that 'new' feeling. But Fred Astaire had a different solution. 'To get that stiff squareness out of it,' he explained, 'I often take a brand-new suit or hat and throw it up against a wall a few times.'

WAISTCOATS

'The King hath yesterday ... declared his resolution of setting a fashion for clothes which he will never alter,' wrote Pepys in his diary on 8 October 1666. 'It will be a vest, I know not well how.'

After the Great Plague and the Great Fire of London, King Charles II was easily persuaded that there was divine displeasure at the extravagant behaviour of his court and country. So, in place of the ever-changing, lavish French fashions of the day, he sought a more permanent, moral and sober dress, and turned to a garment which derived from Persia. The new 'vest' was to be thigh length, and cover up all sight of undergarments under plain material. 'It is to teach the nobility thrift,' wrote Pepys, 'and will do good.'

To insult the new English fashion, Louis XIV put his footmen into vests. But within four years the new fashion had spread across the Continent, and had become firmly established among the nobility. Perhaps, though, this had something to do with the fact that notions of thrift and sobriety were swiftly forgotten. Vests became one of the most decorated items in the male wardrobe, and Louis XIV himself eventually owned one bearing 816 gems. They became waistcoats proper when they were shortened above the abdomen in an eighteenth-century display of masculinity; Regency dandies would wear two at once, the upper unbuttoned to reveal the lower. King George IV reputedly owned 300 decorated in silk and brocade.

But when Charles Dickens went on an American tour in 1842 his bright, decorated waistcoats were criticised as being 'somewhat in the flash order'. By the end of the nineteenth century Oscar Wilde was complaining: 'I find an ever-growing difficulty in expressing my originality through my choice of waistcoats and cravats.'

Yet, despite the pressures of the cloth shortages of the Second World War and the advent of central heating, the waistcoat has survived. So, too, has the rule that the bottom button must always be worn undone – perhaps because the original full-length vests had to be left unbuttoned for walking, or perhaps, as popular legend has it, because Edward VII, while Prince of Wales, inadvertently left his undone, and everyone followed suit to avoid embarrassment. And the word 'vest' has survived too, not only in American speech, but in the way that Savile Row tailors refer to the garment.

Pop go the waistcoats – one of the privileges of belonging to Pop, the self-electing élite among Eton pupils, is the right to wear patterned waistcoats. The results, like the pupils themselves, are in a class of their own.

Fancy silk waistcoats, 'somewhat in the flash order'.

Formal day in double-breasted grey

Plain grey, for town and around.

Scoop lapels – right for the night.

Classic country – check the pattern and flaps.

City pretty – smart but artful.

JACKETS

'The jacket is different from the knickerbockers, but the effect is a harmony rather than a contrast.' With that remark, a contemporary commentator attempted to explain to puzzled gentlemen of the 1920s the notion of a sports jacket.

It seems odd that the sports jacket should be such a recent introduction into the wardrobe. But before country pastimes became popular in the late nineteenth century there was really no call for something which was neither part of a suit, nor of formal dress. And when country walking and shooting first became popular, tweed suits were the order of the day.

It was the Norfolk jacket which changed the pattern of menswear. Tradition links it to the sportsmen on the Duke of Norfolk's estate, where guests included the Prince of Wales (later King George IV). And some say it was the Prince himself who ordered a garment from his tailors which would make it easier to swing a gun than in tailored suit coats. The Norfolk design not only has a loose, comfortable fit across shoulders and chest; it also has box pleats, two in the front and one in the rear, which open and close as the wearer swivels around. It was a garment specifically designed, rather than adapted, for use in sports – and it was a waist-length coat which did not match the trousers.

But it was not until the 1920s that sports jackets without those functional elements began to be worn for other activities. As the lounge suit began to replace formal dress for business, so the tweed jacket and flannels became accepted casual dress.

Jacket in – Dirk Bogarde displays the fashionable modern style of the separate sports jacket.

Jacket out –
Today the wool sports jacket has replaced the Norfolk for outdoor country wear.

S A F A R I J A C K E T

What the big game hunters of the 1920s needed was a garment sturdy enough to survive in the bush, but light enough to be wearable in a 100-degree equatorial climate. It also had to be washable, and have enough pockets to carry essential survival equipment. The solution was created by the legendary Manhattan sporting store Abercrombie & Fitch, with expedition outfitters Willis & Geiger. That original safari jacket, model 486, made of cotton woven 340 strands to the inch (three times as dense as standard fabric) is still made today. And so are twelve other models, including 476, which Ernest Hemingway helped design for himself and which has an additional pocket on the arm – for his spectacles.

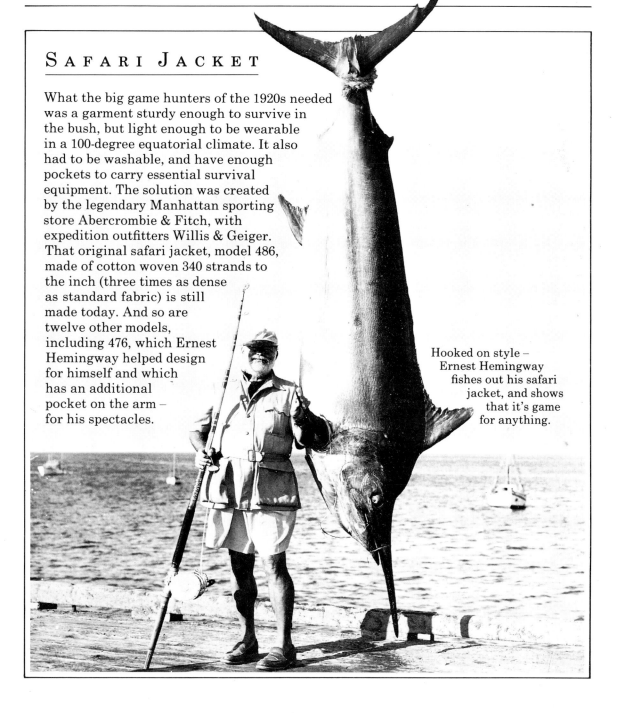

Hooked on style – Ernest Hemingway fishes out his safari jacket, and shows that it's game for anything.

TWEED

The classic country cloth

Contrary to popular opinion, tweed has nothing to do with the River Tweed. Its name comes from a nineteenth-century clerk who wrote out an invoice for a consignment of twill, or 'tweel' to the Scots, being sent from Hawick to London. The word was mistaken for 'tweed' – and the name stuck.

Woven in hard, working areas, woollen tweeds like Cheviot, Irish, Scottish, Yorkshire and Saxony became the first choice among Victorian and Edwardian country gentlemen. And the rugged fabrics have remained ideal for the British climate. Some are distinguished by their looks – Irish tweed has a white warp and a dark filling, and Donegal tweed is flecked with colours to produce the 'pepper and salt'

'Of all manly dresses', according to Jane Austen's Marianne Dashwood, 'a shooting jacket was the most becoming.'

It was a sign of wealth to have a separate jacket for 'sports'. And soon they were being bought as leisure wear even by City businessmen. For, 'in casting away clothes worn during working hours, the cares and worries of the daily round fly with them; a change of raiment makes a new man of one'.

Echoing its country origins, the English sports jacket has always been heavier than a suit coat, made in tweed or wool, and differentiated by its details. The pockets can be in the more casual patch style, or with the pleats and bellows designed to accommodate gun cartridges, flasks and the like. Hacking pockets, angled for easy access while horse-riding, can also be worn. The buttons may be

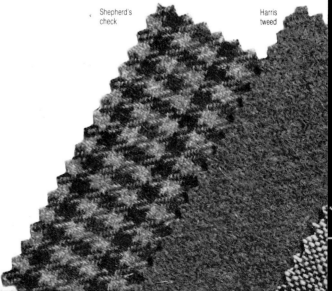

Shepherd's check

Harris tweed

Growing popularity – Sir Terence Conran displays the tweed jacket in its natural Habitat.

effect, while Cheviot tweed has the warp and filling dyed the same colour, often the moss green of country suits.

But one tweed is distinguished by its reputation. In 1844 the Earl of Dunmore encouraged the hand-weavers on the Scottish island he owned to copy a pattern of the Murray tartan in their local tweed. His Countess then improved the patterns, and encouraged the use of local dyes – and now Harris Tweed is the most famous of all tweeds. Colourful and enormously hard wearing, only the wool still hand-woven on the Islands of the Outer Hebrides, including Lewis and Harris itself, is entitled to the cherished label.

Patched with leather on elbows and cuffs, a tweed jacket will give years of service. But although worn now in both town and country, tweed remains resolutely informal. Lord Harris once tried to break with tradition by wearing a tweed suit into the Royal Enclosure at Ascot, in place of morning dress. 'Mornin', Harris,' he was greeted by King Edward VII. 'Goin' rattin'?'

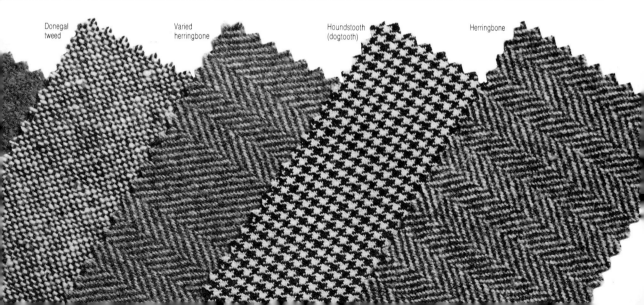

Donegal tweed

Varied herringbone

Houndstooth (dogtooth)

Herringbone

THE BLAZER

The origin of the blazer goes back to the Captain of the frigate *HMS Blazer*, who in 1837 was faced with a visit to his ship by Queen Victoria. To smarten up his shabby-looking crew the Captain had short jackets in navy blue serge, with brass Royal Navy buttons, made up for his men. Queen Victoria was so impressed by the crew's appearance that the jackets became a permanent part of their dress.

Thicker, heavier 'reefer' jackets had been worn previously by midshipmen, who hauled in the sails (or 'reefs'). Some think these may have inspired the Captain's design; certainly their double-breasted front has been carried on to the classic blazer. Today, the naval blazer also retains its uniform navy colour, although more versatile blazers are now made from flannel rather than serge. The brass buttons also remain, to carry either military, club or college crests, or nautical emblems; if buttons are plain, then they should be flat, whereas crested buttons should be semi-spherical. A naval blazer has flap pockets, but all three pockets on a sporting or school blazer are patch; the breast is a patch (instead of the more usual welt) in order to carry a crest, and the side pockets should match.

Coloured and striped summer blazers took their name in the last century from the bright red jackets worn by the oarsmen of Lady Margaret Boat Club, Cambridge, which were said to look 'ablaze'. These are traditionally single-breasted; made up in club or College colours, they are still only worn at outdoor sporting events such as Henley Royal Regatta.

Trail blazer – Richard Branson wears the classic blue double-breasted with a touch of gilt.

The crests of the waves are the most appropriate for blazer pockets and buttons. Yacht and rowing clubs are followed by college and regimental crests, embroidered in heavy gold wire, with hemispherical crested buttons in brass or gilt keeping to the original Navy uniform tradition.

Ablaze in club colours at the Henley Regatta, where boaters are as essential as the boats.

leather and, instead of the plain 'bluff' edge of a suit coat, a sports jacket may have a 'swelled' edge, with a row of stitching about a quarter of an inch from the edge running around the front, bottom edge, collar and lapels. And it can be patched, with leather, at the elbows and cuffs. All of these make the informal sports jacket distinct from the formal suit coat.

As the idea of the separate jacket spread abroad, lighter materials were adopted elsewhere to suit warmer climates. Seersucker was popular with plantation owners in the southern USA; a cool blend of Orlon polyester with cotton, it can be washed and worn without pressing. It takes its name from the Hindu word 'shirushaker' meaning 'puckered', describing its distinctive finish, and in a blue and white stripe it has become an American classic. Cotton poplin, madras, and linen are also used now for lightweight jackets. But because of the climate, the traditional English jacket is always heavier than a suit.

The informality of the jacket also offers an opportunity for more distinct patterns than on formal suits. Even the Duke of Windsor admitted that 'I believe in bright checks for sportsmen. The louder they are,' he said, 'the better I like them.' And the traditional patterns for sports jackets are also the boldest, named after the animal characteristics they resemble – houndstooth check and herringbone. The straight Shepherd's check is sometimes worn on its own, but more often underlies other checks and plaids, while the soft patterns and mottled pepper and salt effects of many tweeds have made them country favourites. The designer Hardy Amies expressed it perfectly; the ideal is a distinctive pattern, planned 'in such a way that the traditional is not obscured by the fantastic.'

HATS

One of the ways of spotting a true gentleman, it was said, was to observe the first thing that he did on entering a house. If he took his hat off he was probably a gentleman. If he did not take his hat off he was only pretending to be a gentleman. And if he had no hat on his head in the first place, then there was no gentlemanliness about him, in fact or in pretence.

Low-roofed cars, the ugliness of the demob hat, the fashion for long hair and the fact that President Kennedy went bare-headed, were all blamed for the demise of the hat in the 1960s. But now the hatters of St James's are brimming over with confidence that the classic designs are making a comeback.

Top hat

The top hat was first worn on 15 January 1797 by John Hetherington, a hat-maker in the Strand. The date is known so precisely because four women fainted, passers-by booed, and a small boy broke his arm in the excitement. Hetherington was arrested, and charged with causing a breach of the peace, by wearing 'a tall structure having a shiny lustre calculated to alarm timid people'. He was bound over in the sum of £500 not to repeat the offence.

Yet in the nineteenth century the top hat became the most popular style of all. Sadly it is now worn only on the most formal occasions, correct with any style of tailcoat.

From the toffs in toppers to the chaps in caps, with the blokes in Cokes standing somewhere in between. There was a time when a hat was a sure sign of social position, and an uncovered head was an uncommon sight. Now, it's hair there and everywhere.

STRAW HAT

The straw hat began life with butchers, as a light, cool hat which protected their heads from dripping blood. Yet they became more common at the other end of the social scale, as the riverside hat for Henley (hence 'boater'), and as part of public school uniform. Under the school regulations at Winchester College boys had to wear their straw hats (or 'strats' as they called them) to all lessons. They were only allowed to remove them on their first day (to identify themselves as new boys) and in chapel, when they would leave them outside. But in 1983 strats were abolished, and 600 years of tradition came sadly to an end.

BOWLER

When high-crowned toppers were all the rage, William Coke went to Lock's to commission something more suitable for his gamekeepers – and they created a low, hard hat made of rabbit skin and shellac, designed to be more practical under low-hanging branches. It became known as a bowler when a firm of that name started making them; but in Lock's they are still known as Cokes.

Between the wars 7,000 bowlers were being made every year, and it became a symbol of the London businessman. 'It should never be worn abroad,' says Hardy Amies, 'never by foreigners, and Americans who attempt to do so should be fined.'

TRILBY

Its name comes from George du Maurier's novel of 1894, a book so popular that its title was applied to several different items of clothing, although only the trilby hat has survived. Like most classic hats it has the traditional hat band, with a tiny bow on the left hand side – a vestige of the plume of the Cavaliers, which always had to be worn on the opposite side to their sword hand.

FEDORA

The fedora takes its name from Princess Fedora Romanoff, a character in a Victorian melodrama written for Sarah Bernhardt and first performed in 1883. Its flexible brim can be worn up or snapped down; hence its nickname – a 'snap brim'. And that brim is rather wider than that of its close relative, the trilby, giving the fedora a more flamboyant and artistic style.

DEERSTALKER

Perhaps the most distinctive country hat of all, with its heavily stitched, six-piece centre button crown and jutting brim. The tweed deerstalker is equally correct with or without ear flaps, which can be tied on top of the hat or worn down over the ears in cold weather. You don't have to be a detective to realise why such a practical design has remained a country favourite.

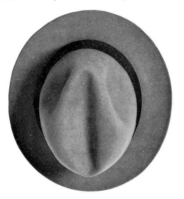

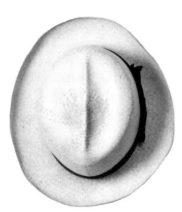

PANAMA (OPTIMO CROWN)

Panama hats actually came from the hills of Ecuador, but they got their name from sailors who stopped off at the coast on their way up to the Californian gold rush. The original versions had a full 'optimo' crown, with a ridge running from back to front, which helped in folding up the hat. The test of a fine Panama was said to be whether it could be folded and then passed through a wedding ring.

PANAMA (FLAT CROWN)

The English took to the cool, light and unlined Panamas for summer wear, but they preferred them with a more conventional crown. In either style, the hats were traditionally made from a soft, South American reed. And the best were reputedly made underwater, which was supposed to preserve the silky feel of the reeds until the hat was actually finished.

FLAT CAP (SHORT PEAK)

In 1571 an Act of Parliament ordained that on Sundays and holidays all males over six years of age, except for the nobility and persons of degree, were to wear caps of wool manufactured in England, on force of a fine of 3/4d a day. This bid to stimulate trade was not repealed until 1597; by then flat woollen caps were already recognised as the mark of a citizen, tradesman or apprentice.

BROWN TRILBY

Somerset Maugham once scathingly dismissed someone with the damning description, 'He's the kind of fellow who wears a brown hat in London.' The brown trilby has always been a country hat, worn with tweeds and corduroys, and it is still popular with the racing fraternity. But although it is no longer quite such a social gaffe, a brown hat is still not appropriate in town.

HOMBURG

Proper for day or evening wear, the black or midnight blue homburg is the most formal of hats after the topper, and for that reason it is still worn by heads of state and diplomats today. It takes its name from the German spa town and resort where it first appeared; King Edward VII discovered it there, and he popularised its roll-brim, side-curl style in England.

FLAT CAP (LONG PEAK)

Now, country gentlemen have adopted the longer-peaked 'shooting cap', and the cap with the clip-down peak and crown button, known in parts of the country as a 'rattin' 'at', but also called a Windsor cap. It has enjoyed a huge change in social status since 1906, when Keir Hardie, the first Labour MP, wore his flat cap when elected to Parliament, as a gesture of working-class solidarity.

BOATER

The straw hat has successfully spanned the classes, from the working butcher, through the riverside oarsman, past the song-and-dance entertainers like Maurice Chevalier and Frankie Vaughan, to the top of Britain's public schools. Surprisingly tough for such a light, cool hat, a boater which has passed several summers will lose its initial garish gold, and gain a deep, biscuit-coloured suntan.

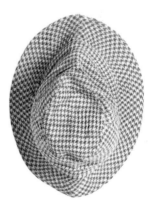

FISHING HAT

Some call them simply sports hats; they've been made in corduroy and in cotton (known as 'beanie hats'), while some country chaps insist that they're really grouse hats. But the floppy tweed hat, with a flat crown, is most widely known as a fisherman's hat, because it provides an ideal place to hook on fishing flies. It's the only hat which can be carried as comfortably in a pocket as on a head.

OVERCOATS

'I am only conscious of it,' said one of Victor Hugo's characters, 'because it keeps me warm.' Today, there are only certain styles of overcoat which can be so discreetly effective.

A handful of overcoats have survived as classics, and the most formal is the Chesterfield, named after the nineteenth-century Earl of Chesterfield. Based on the design of the frock coat but not cut in at the waist, it was always intended as a formal coat. Cut double- or single-breasted, from about 1850 the fly-front opening came into fashion, and this has remained a feature of the single-breasted version, whether made up in a fine grey herringbone or a plain blue, black or beige. (Gentlemen, it seems, do not, like Joseph, wear coats of many colours.)

The Chesterfield often has a black velvet

The classic Chesterfield in herringbone wool, with a black velvet collar and a fly front to conceal the buttons when done up, as worn by John Singer Sargent.

Acting up – Prime Minister Winston Churchill in an astrakhan coat, more commonly associated with theatrical figures. Collar and cuffs are made from curly Russian lambswool.

collar. This dates back to the French Revolution, when the gentlemen in other coun-
tries who wanted to show their sympathy
with the executed bourgeoisie added a black
collar to their coats as a mark of sympathy.
It soon became an upper-class fashion, and
still has a place on the most formal coats
today. (The black astrakhan collar, on the
other hand, has always had a rather spivvy
image. True astrakhan is a curly fur, which
comes from young lambs in the Astrakhan
region of Russia. Today most astrakhan
fabric is an imitation, and most astrakhan
wearers are equally suspect. Even Churchill
was accused of wearing a coat better suited
to a theatrical impresario.)

The Chesterfield and other formal coats
have cut-in sleeves; raglan sleeves, which are

True blue – the Crombie overcoat is made of
exceptionally thick, rich wool, and is
traditionally dyed a dark blue colour. It's now
one of the most popular City coats.

Warm shoulder – the epaulettes betray the
military heritage of the British Warm. Equally
distinctive are the brown leather buttons and
fawn colour.

THE DUFFLE COAT

Perhaps the only coat capable of keeping The Cruel Sea out of Jack Hawkins's bones was the duffle. The name derives from Duffel, a town in Belgium, and as long ago as the eighteenth century Defoe says that duffel, 'a coarse woollen stuff', was exported to the New World. But the hooded coat of Tyrolean cloth, fastened with wooden toggles and hemp loops (ideal for frozen fingers) really came into its own when it was adopted by the Royal Navy. In the Second World War it also became known as a 'convoy coat', and after it was popularised by Field Marshal Montgomery, it gained its European nickname of a 'Monty coat'. Cheap, surplus stock was released to the public in the 1950s, and the duffle became a warm favourite.

cut with seams that extend from shoulder to neck, always make a coat more casual. Legend traces this design back to the first Baron Raglan, hero of the Crimean War; to keep his soldiers warm he devised a garment made from a potato sack, slit at the neck and slashed diagonally across the corners to allow the arms to swing free. This diagonal opening forms the basis for the raglan sleeve design and its comfortable, easy cut.

Ease of movement also dictated that the British Warm, which was a military coat, and the covert coat, the classic country coat, are cut shorter than town coats. The covert coat takes its name from its twilled lightweight cloth, usually now a lovat wool, woven to give a 'mixed' effect and first used as a hunting fabric. Along with country pursuits, the covert coat's popularity took off around 1890, and it has remained popular in the country. A traditional covert has four lines of stitching around the base and cuffs, known to some tailors as 'railroading'; it is also one of the few overcoats with a breast pocket.

The British Warm, a distinctive design in fawn melton wool, with brown leather buttons and epaulettes, made its first appearance on the Indian frontier, when the British troops faced a hard long winter during the Tirah Campaign. Cut short and double-breasted, it could accept a fleecy lining in its easy cut. Officers wore a longer, belted version, with a deep collar, the forerunner of other overcoat designs. After the war the version worn by the troops was adapted for civilian use.

The ideal overcoat is cut rather loose; Dr Johnson's 'might almost have held the two volumes of his folio dictionary'. Wool and cashmere remain the ideal fabrics; genuine camelhair is now rare, and the term describes a colour more often than a cloth. The soft crombie wool, and the heavy melton (which first came into general use in the town of Melton Mowbray), are materials which will give several years service. 'Old coats are just like old friends,' concluded Hugo's character; a classic style in quality material still provides an opportunity to find out why.

THE BARBOUR

John Barbour went into business in 1890, producing his waterproof, thornproof jackets. The company's first catalogue offered its Beacon Brand, 'absolutely waterproof special light weight coat, popular for many years with officers of the Merchant Navy'. And now, the range of waxed cotton jackets goes from the 24-oz Durham, through the middleweight Border, to the heavy senior model, the Solway Zipper. They are now the emblem of country gentlemen everywhere, and known simply as the Barbour.

The design of the Barbour has been copied by hosts of imitators, and has become the classic country gentleman's jacket. Waxed cotton is light, tough and waterproof, and its traditional olive colour is the perfect countryside camouflage. The outer pockets are capacious bellows pockets (see p. 30). Storm cuffs, with an interior elasticated cuff shielded by the outer cotton sleeve, afford added waterproofing at the wrists, while a storm fly front shields a two-way zip. A 'poacher's pocket', which runs around the base but on the inside of the jacket, is waterproof, washable and less immediately detectable than bulging outer pockets. Some Barbours also have 'handwarmers', two pockets thoughtfully lined with moleskin: Beneath the corduroy faced collar a genuine Barbour has studs to attach a separate hood. And beneath the distinctive exterior is the traditional tartan body liner.

But what sets the original Barbour apart? Barbour proudly draw attention to the fact that their product is made only from 'finest long-staple Egyptian cotton', and constructed from forty pieces of material with over 15,000 stitches. Their solid brass press fastenings have a corrosion proof oxidized finish, and a self-locating ball and socket mechanism. Their records include personal testimonials such as the man who lost his Barbour over the side of a boat on Lake Windermere. Eight months later it was dredged up; after a good hosing it was returned to Barbour for reproofing, and is back in active service today. And their jackets carry that most respected recommendation, the crested announcement which proclaims that Barbours are made By Royal Appointment to both the Duke of Edinburgh and the Prince of Wales.

RAINCOATS

Charles Macintosh never intended to make raincoats. In 1822 he patented his 'India rubber cloth', which was actually two pieces of material sandwiched together with rubber softened by naptha. The waterproof cloth was a great success for tarpaulins and the like. The only problem was that tailors rushed to make coats from it, despite Macintosh's warning that if they sewed the material the needle-holes would let in water. The tailors persisted, and their coats duly leaked. In an effort to get it right, they made them with double-stitched seams; the coats let in twice as much water. By this time the new waterproof fabric was being scorned; the only way for Macintosh to preserve the reputation of his invention was to open retail shops himself and employ staff to make coats with properly proofed seams. These were the first truly waterproof coats; with a tartan lining, appropriate to his Scottish origins, the traditional raincoat was born, and naturally took on its creator's name.

Rubber macintoshes were never the ideal raincoats: the non-porous material smells, it encourages perspiration, and it is difficult to tailor. But Macintosh's fabric was, as claimed, completely waterproof. So while modern proofing methods eventually allowed other materials to be used for raincoats, rubberised fabrics have stayed in use for working garments and capes. In 1851 a London manufacturer, George Spill, invented the idea of using metal eyelets under the armpits, 'forming an outlet for perspiration, thus obviating the principal objection against the use of waterproof apparel'. These are still used today in 'macs' and oilskins.

THE BURBERRY

When Captain Alcock first flew the Atlantic he did it in a Burberry. 'Although in continual mist, rain or sleet,' he wrote, 'I kept as dry, warm and comfortable as possible under such conditions. This was a wonderful achievement even for Burberrys'.'

Thomas Burberry of Hampshire was once told by a doctor that the ideal waterproof would be one which would withstand wind and rain, but allow the body to breathe. Inspired by the closely woven linen smocks of local shepherds, he designed a cotton material proofed both in the yarn and then again in the piece. He called the material gabardine; the coats he made from it became known by his name after King Edward habitually asked his staff to 'Give me my Burberry'.

During the Boer War officers began to wear Burberry weatherproofs for active service. The War Office gave its official approval, and the specifically designed coat for trench warfare made its appearance in 1914. All the authentic details remain: the storm flap on one shoulder, the epaulettes, and the D-rings on the belt (used to clip on military equipment). A total of 500,000 military Burberrys were worn by combatants in the Great War, and the Trench '21' model is still available today. Lord Kitchener died in a Burberry; and it was a tent made of exactly the same Burberry gabardine which took Amundsen to the Pole and was left there as the mark of his conquest.

BURBERRY TRENCH-WARM

Rain supreme –
the trenchcoat is
equally at home
in Cornhill
or Casablanca.

TROUSERS

It is hard to believe that, until the French Revolution, gentlemen would wear only pantaloons, and considered trousers to be working wear suitable only for sailors. The Duke of Wellington was turned away from the famous Almack's gambling club in London for attempting to enter in trousers. Today, he would be turned away for attempting to enter in anything else.

CUT

Dismissing fads such as bell-bottoms, drainpipes and peg-tops, there are two classic trouser cuts – the straight leg and the naturally tapered leg. The very first trousers were cut extremely close, and fashions have varied ever since, but as man has retained his natural taper from hip to ankle, so there is a good argument for his trousers doing the same. At the bottom, the trouser has traditionally been tailored so that it covers three-quarters of the length of the shoe.

FRONT

The trouser front can be either plain or pleated. Pleats were introduced to accommodate wider cuts of trouser; at the time of the baggiest 'peg-top' trousers several pleats were needed to draw all the material into the waistband. Classic trousers should just have two, one which becomes the front crease, and another midway between the first pleat and the pocket. These allow the trousers to respond to the hips when sitting, they break up the width of the trouser front, and they allow the cloth to drape elegantly.

Pleated-front trousers are more elegant, but they do require a fuller cut in the thigh so that the pleats do not pull open when standing. If trousers are cut close to the leg, then a plain front must be used.

WAISTBAND

The style of the waistband depends on whether the trousers are to be worn with a

OXFORD BAGS

It was in the hot summer of 1925 that Oxford Bags first appeared. In his *Memoirs of an Aesthete* Harold Acton claimed the entire credit for their invention: 'I wore jackets with broad lapels', he wrote, 'and broad pleated trousers. The latter got broader and broader. Eventually they were imitated elsewhere and generally referred to as "Oxford Bags".' But the baggy trousers are more commonly believed to have their origin in the loose, towelling trousers worn by oarsmen over their shorts. Helped by their contrast to the slim, elegant trousers of the old guard, they became the height of fashion, and 'even caught the Speaker's eye'. But after getting baggier and baggier, with bottoms in some cases of 40 in, they were taken in as quickly

ANOTHER BLOW FOR OXFORD.

as they had been taken up, banished by ridicule and by the bad example of Oxford's longest-ever series of successive defeats in the Boat Race.

belt or braces. This has only recently become an option; the rule has always been that formal wear demands braces, but they are inappropriate for casual or sports dress. So trousers which are not sold as part of a suit, and are therefore casual, are often fitted with belt loops.

If braces are to be worn, the waist should be 1 in larger than on belted trousers, to allow them to hang properly. The original style of formal and suit trousers has buttons outside the waistband with the rear of the trousers raised in a V, to accommodate braces. But modern tailors put all buttons on the inside of the waistband, which also permits the use of clip-on braces. Versatility suggests this latter style, tradition the former; modernity that we should all belt up.

CREASE

The only trousers which can be worn today without a crease are jeans, which should never have one. Yet trousers did not originally have a crease, and when Edward VII invented them they were side creases, formed by the way his trousers were folded for storage. His son and heir George did wear front creases, though; after the First World War they became a symbol of the young generation, and when trousers widened in the 1920s they became the necessity they have remained, to show and maintain the line of the trousers. Trousers are the correct length when the crease 'breaks' on the shoe.

To locate a crease correctly, line up the leg seams, then lay the trouser leg flat. The crease is precisely half-way between the two seams.

TURNUPS

For some time after the introduction of trousers men had rolled up the bottoms to keep them out of mud and water. In the early 1890s

this sporting country look was first tailored on to town trousers, to a critical response. There was an uproar in the House when Viscount Lewisham appeared wearing turnups in 1893. However by the early years of this century they had become an accepted variation on regular trouser bottoms. Turned-up bottoms should be cut parallel to the ground, and are ideally worn on trousers with pleated tops; their added weight can produce a more elegant hang.

Plain bottoms should be cut at a slant, so that they are lower at the heel. The very best are then hemmed inside the bottom with bias binding, which protects against wear, and provides a fraction more weight to improve the hang.

MATERIAL

Flannel, whose name derives from the Welsh *gwlanen* meaning woollen article, is a loosely woven and dully finished weave which shot to popularity with the comfortably-cut trousers of the 1920s. Soft and easy-going, yet elegantly tailored, grey flannels were originally intended for the summer,

Seam work – the distinctive beaded seam on the outer leg characterises a pair of casual trousers.

an ideal partner for the blazer. Yet in 1938 it was estimated that 70 per cent of men chose to wear flannel throughout the year, in suits as well as trousers. Douglas Fairbanks Jr said he was 'at his best' in flannels, and they remain the most versatile trousers available.

At the other end of formality, apart from corduroy and denim, the two sportiest materials for trousers are Bedford cord, a twill woven with a lengthwise rib, and cavalry twill, which has a 63-degree diagonal rib. These strong and resilient trousers are often used for riding, and country colours, such as rust and moss, predominate. They can be 'beaded', which means the side seams are raised, which gives a more casual appear-

ance. (Beaded trousers should only be worn with a sports jacket, never as part of a suit.)

The most popular cotton trousers have now become known by their American name, 'chinos'. These were originally woven in Manchester, and exported to China, but the Chinese then sold the supplies back to Americans stationed in The Philippines just before the Second World War – hence the name. These comfortable casual trousers have become classic summer wear.

POCKETS

'God gave us no towns; nor did He give us pockets,' wrote the designer Hardy Amies. 'We can therefore place them where they are

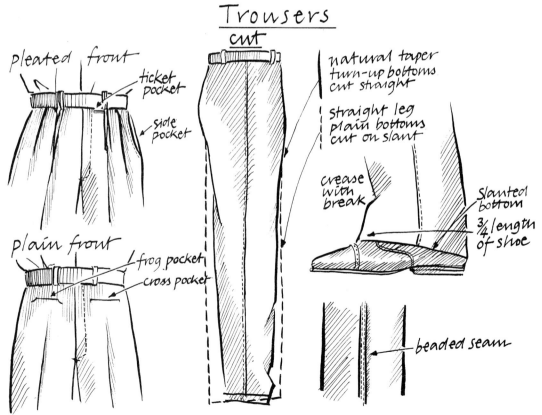

Trousers cut

pleated front
ticket pocket
side pocket

plain front
frog pocket
cross pocket

natural taper turn-up bottoms cut straight

straight leg plain bottoms cut on slant

crease with break

Slanted bottom
3/4 length of shoe

beaded seam

CORDUROY

Corduroy is literally *corde du roi*, the King's cord. It was the material used on the hunting livery of the servants of the King of France, and once the ribs were cut by hand, one at a time, and then brushed to raise the pile. From these origins, however, it became known as a poor man's velvet, because its pile is made of cotton rather than silk or satin. And in the late nineteenth century Sydney Webb could declare that 'corduroy has been relegated to the use of navvies and tramps'. Fortunately the warmth and comfort of corduroy was recognised and rescued – and now the question of its popularity is particularly academic.

Wale educated – the ribs in corduroy are properly known as 'wales' (from the Anglo-Saxon *walu* meaning to flail with stripes), and vary from the narrow pinwale to the broader wide wale.

most convenient to us.' Originally cross pockets, cut parallel with the waist, were the most convenient, because they were usable while riding. But as man came down to earth so his pockets were relocated on either thigh, coupled with hip pockets at the rear, neither of which would be convenient on horseback. When trousers became tighter cut in the 1960s, there was a return to cross pockets, 'frogmouthed' for easier access. But cross pockets cannot be worn with pleated fronts, and the only remaining cross pocket today should be the ticket pocket, cut into the waist.

It is a sign of well-made trousers that the material is taken far enough into the pockets so that the pocket lining does not show when sitting down. If the pockets gape open when standing, the trousers are cut too tightly across the rear.

FLIES

Despite the fact that Earl Mountbatten was among the first to adopt them in 1934, zip flies were mistrusted for decades. Not only was there the risk of coming open, but also of shutting painfully. There is one Savile Row tailor who remembers, when he was an apprentice, a customer phoning in to complain about the newfangled device. The horrified apprentice passed on to his boss the message that, after trapping himself in the zip, the customer had required five stitches. His boss looked up from his work and said simply, 'Boastful bugger!'

Most flies now have nylon zips, which rarely stick, but a trick for loosening a metal zip is to run a pencil up and down the join of the teeth. The graphite in the pencil lead acts as a lubricant.

JEANS

Among the many who rushed to San Francisco in 1850 to try their luck in the Gold Rush was a twenty-year-old Bavarian immigrant who thought there might be money in supplying canvas tents to the gold-diggers. But when he arrived he found they were more concerned about their trousers, which lasted no time at all in 'the diggins'. So, in order to make use of the tenting canvas, he turned the material into the 'waist-high overall'. And the tough new trousers sold so well that the immigrant was able to open a shop selling them under his own name – Levi Strauss.

Levi's trousers were soon being made in a durable cotton, woven in the South of France, and known as *serge de Nîmes*, colloquialised into 'denim'. The word 'jeans' is believed to have come from the 'Genoese', the Italian sailors who wore blue denim on their trading ships. And the essential character of denim jeans was completed in 1873, when a Nevada tailor suggested to Levi the use of rust-proof copper rivets to strengthen the pocket seams.

Traditional jeans like Levi's 501s use $14\frac{1}{2}$-oz heavy-weight denim; its deep indigo colour comes from an eight-dip dyeing process which builds up layers of colour on the yarn. Over a period of wearing and washing the jeans 'shrink-to-fit', the fabric 'blooms', and the colour fades half a shade lighter. It all adds up to the particularly individual character of blue denim jeans, perhaps the only garment whose claim to perfection is that they are guaranteed to wrinkle, shrink and fade.

~the miner
farmer, mechanic and cattle raiser
all over the west prefer
cut full –
honestly made –
Levi Strauss & Co's.
copper riveted Overalls
the most persistently advertised – the best selling brand. it will pay you to handle them.

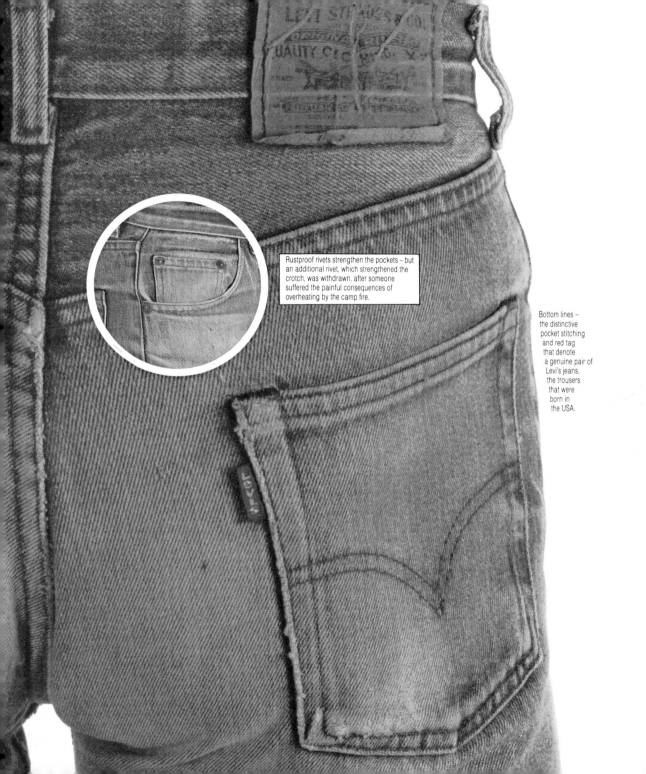

Rustproof rivets strengthen the pockets – but an additional rivet, which strengthened the crotch, was withdrawn, after someone suffered the painful consequences of overheating by the camp fire.

Bottom lines – the distinctive pocket stitching and red tag that denote a genuine pair of Levi's jeans, the trousers that were born in the USA.

FOOTWEAR

On his fiftieth birthday in 1971 Prince Philip received a letter of congratulation on his longevity. He wrote back a letter of thanks and added, 'One of the reasons I am going so well must be that I have always been well shod.'

History has seen a continuing social battle between boots and shoes. The high boots of the seventeenth century gave way to the buckled shoes of the eighteenth, before the Wellington and other boots came back into vogue in the early nineteenth century. (The Wellington, as worn by the Iron Duke, was actually a knee-high leather boot, distinguished from others because the top was not turned down; the rubber version was not introduced until early this century.) So boots, whether laced, buttoned or elastic-sided, were all popular in Victorian times.

But back in the eighteenth century the first reference to shoes was as 'Oxford-cut'. These shoes, fashionable at the University, were cut below the ankle, laced directly up the front arch, and had the quarters (where the laces are carried) stitched *under* the vamp, or front, of the shoe. (The alternative style, with the quarters stitched over the vamp, was known as the Derby.) The Oxford was gradually recognised as the most elegant way to toe the sartorial line.

When Queen Victoria popularised shooting holidays in Scotland the Oxford brogue

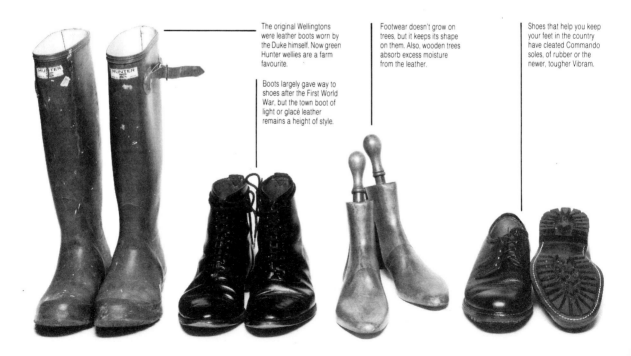

The original Wellingtons were leather boots worn by the Duke himself. Now green Hunter wellies are a farm favourite.

Boots largely gave way to shoes after the First World War, but the town boot of light or glacé leather remains a height of style.

Footwear doesn't grow on trees, but it keeps its shape on them. Also, wooden trees absorb excess moisture from the leather.

Shoes that help you keep your feet in the country have cleated Commando soles, of rubber or the newer, tougher Vibram.

suddenly leapt in popularity. Brogues were a development from the original *brog*, the Gaelic for shoe, a basic kind of heavy footwear worn in the wilder parts of the Scottish Highlands, and made from tanned cowhide rubbed with melted tallow. The *brog* was pierced with holes to allow the water of the bogs to pass in and out of the shoe. These heavy Scottish country shoes were duplicated in a lighter style; 'broguing' became a purely decorative pattern of punched holes and pinking and, by the 1930s, Oxford brogues and semi-brogues had become the most fashionable kinds of footwear. (The semi-brogue is a shoe whose broguing is restricted to the toe-cap alone; the full

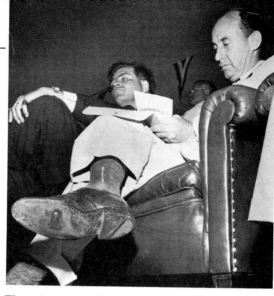

The sole result of a hard slog along the Presidential campaign trail, accidentally revealed by Adlai Stevenson. The photo made him an instant folk hero. Governor Stevenson just remarked drily 'Better a hole in the shoe than a hole in the head.'

Full, single brogues are the way a City gentleman comes down to earth in a patterned but acceptably sober style.

The best of both worlds: plain and pattern meet in the semi-brogue, with the punching restricted to the toe-cap of the shoe.

Full, double country brogues: with heavier construction and wider welt, they're closer to the original *brog*.

The Duke of Windsor was the first to wear reversed calf shoes with a suit; nowadays, gentlemen are more easily suede.

brogue has broguing that extends to the sides of the shoe. Full brogues are called 'wing-tips' by Americans, because the toe decoration resembles a bird with spread wings and American shoe makers also make 'long' wing-tips, where the brogue follows round to the heel. The other distinction is between single brogues, consisting of uppers and sole, and double brogues, which have a welt between the two.)

In recent years the moccasin has also entered the English wardrobe. A true moccasin completely wraps the foot in two pieces of leather: one, face-down, is beneath the foot, but rises to form the sides of the shoe, while the other piece, face up, forms the top or 'vamp' of the shoe. The European moccasin, popularised by Aldo Gucci's design, decorates the instep of the shoe with a metal snaffle, but the American version, the 'loafer', is decorated with a discreet leather strip, or 'saddle'. The English have favoured the tasselled loafer, but the classic American loafers are Bass Weejuns, introduced in the 1930s. These are actually a variation of a shoe made in the off-season by Norwegian fishermen – hence their name, 'weejuns'. But they are also known as 'penny loafers', because Ivy League students used to put a cent, or penny, into the saddle as decoration.

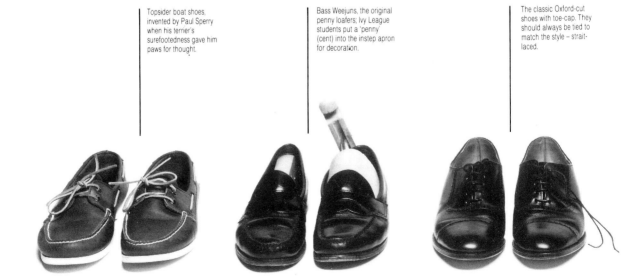

Topsider boat shoes, invented by Paul Sperry when his terrier's surefootedness gave him paws for thought.

Bass Weejuns, the original penny loafers; Ivy League students put a 'penny' (cent) into the instep apron for decoration.

The classic Oxford-cut shoes with toe-cap. They should always be tied to match the style – strait-laced.

The most casual and most formal shoes in the wardrobe (considered fully under Casual and Evening Dress) are boat shoes and evening pumps. Only the suede shoe has a problem finding its place in the spectrum of formality. Suede is properly known as reversed calf – its name is derived from the French word for Sweden, where it originated. The Duke of Windsor once caused a sensation by wearing brown suede shoes with a dark blue suit. But when a bystander expressed surprise at this sartorial *faux pas*, one of the Duke's friends justified it thus: 'It would be wrong if it were a mistake. But the Duke *knows better* – so it's alright.'

SHINING EXAMPLE

For a fine shoeshine a good wax polish should first be applied using a soft rag. Spit lightly on the polish, in the traditional 'spit and polish' method, as it is worked in. Then leave the polish to soak into the first shoe while applying it to the second.

A genuine bristle brush is best for the first polish, using long, light strokes; never scrub at the shoe. And then to finish, an oil-dressed chamois leather (not simulated), folded into a pad, will bring out the deeper shine, and remove any polish that could rub off on to trousers.

English tasselled loafers combine the elegant lines of a gentleman's shoes with the decoration of casual footwear.

The Gucci family claim the invention of the modern moccasin, although the style has been snaffled by others.

Bowing to tradition, pumps are the oldest part of modern evening dress, and toe a classic line in black tie.

Socks

The Charter of Eton College states that neither staff nor boy are 'permitted to wear red, green or white hose'. Peregrine Worsthorne, now the Editor of *The Sunday Telegraph*, achieved notoriety for wearing red socks with his pinstripe suits. David Hockney continues to wear a different colour on each foot. As style-spotter Peter York pointed out, who can say the art of conversation is dead when a man can still make a point with the colour of his socks?

It was the Victorians who insisted that men should wear dark socks. After Rev. William Lee of Nottinghamshire invented a machine to knit socks in 1589 all manner of colours were worn. But the nineteenth century saw a return to more sombre hues. Aspiring gentlemen were advised that in order to survive in society, five different weights of sock were essential – silk, wool, thread, cotton and 'mixture'. White socks were correct only with uniform; otherwise, they should wear nothing but grey and white shotted, or sombre black.

But decoration did break out again after the First World War, when shoes replaced ankle boots. Socks could again be seen, and the embroidered ankle decorations, known as 'clocks', flourished once more.

Now decorated, brightly-coloured and argyle socks are worn once again with sombre suits, as a statement of individuality – a statement as loud as the wearer dares. Argyles, in back, grey and white, have even been seen with evening dress. And there has been a return to the quality of hand-framed socks, with the wool set on the knitting frame and tied off by hand; they can be identified by the knots inside the sock leg.

While wool 'country socks' can now be worn in town, the opposite is still not the case. It remains as Dashiell Hammett's hero observed in *The Glass Key*:

'He was looking at the blond man's outstretched ankles. He said "You oughtn't to wear silk socks with tweeds."

'Madvig raised a leg straight out to look at the ankle. "No? I like the feel of silk."

'"Then lay off tweeds".'

ARGYLE SOCKS

The distinctive diamond pattern on argyle socks is derived from the original hosiery worn with tartans. This was cut from the same cloth as the kilt, but on the bias so that the squares on the kilt became diamonds on the stockings. When shooting in Scotland became fashionable the patterned socks found their way across the border. But the socks have no connection with the Argyll family; they are the wrong tartan, the wrong colours, and even the wrong spelling.

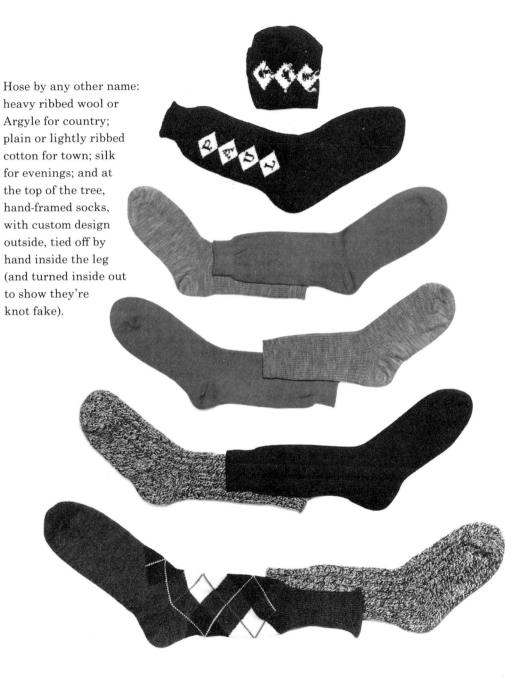

Hose by any other name: heavy ribbed wool or Argyle for country; plain or lightly ribbed cotton for town; silk for evenings; and at the top of the tree, hand-framed socks, with custom design outside, tied off by hand inside the leg (and turned inside out to show they're knot fake).

Underwear

'Underwear', said *Men's Wear* in 1935, 'should have the grace of Apollo, the romance of Byron, the distinction of Lord Chesterfield and the ease, coolness and comfort of Mahatma Gandhi.' It sounds an ideal combination.

Long, Victorian underwear, buttoned at the neck and flies, had few of those characteristics. Yet bolstered by the theories of Dr Jaeger's 'sanitary woollen system', it survived well into this century. But in 1934, inspired by the extremely brief bathing trunks first seen on the French Riviera in 1932, a new design in underpants emerged. It offered (in extraordinary terminology for men's underwear) a 'No-gap opening with gentle support, elastic fibre, no buttons, no bulk, no binding.' In the same year Clark Gable took off his shirt in *It Happened One Night* and revealed that he was not wearing the old, button-up vest. Modern underwear, in the form of briefs alone, was born.

In 1946 Jockey patented the Y-front construction, advertised as 'scientifically perfected for correct masculine support.' And since that opened things up, the shapes and sizes of briefs have proliferated.

Yet recent years have also seen the return of boxer shorts, the design taken literally from the boxing ring which, along with the similarly sport-inspired singlet, first appeared in the 1930s. But are briefs really being relegated to the bottom of the modern wardrobe? The answer is that they will always have good support. And anyway, underwear has long ceased to be any kind of social indicator. As one historian put it, by the end of the First World War, 'its only trace of class distinction was the frequency with which it could be sent to the wash'.

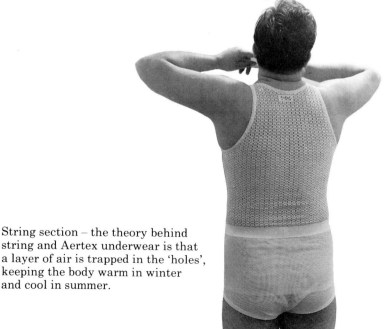

String section – the theory behind string and Aertex underwear is that a layer of air is trapped in the 'holes', keeping the body warm in winter and cool in summer.

Dr. Jaeger's Sanitary Woollen Underclothing—*Continued*.

SANITARY STOCKINGNETTE PANTS,

PATENTED.

BENGER'S MAKE,

Guaranteed Pure Animal Wool,

For MEN, WOMEN and CHILDREN.

The great Sanitary advantages and comfort derived from this soft and durable underclothing are fully described on page 5, to which reference is requested to be made.

These are made of the finest material, afford an agreeable warmth, and are a protection against, and remedy for, disorders of the Stomach, supplying the place of an abdominal bandage.

They are therefore highly approved by the Medical Profession, and can be strongly recommended as a Sanitary form of underclothing.

DOUBLE THICKNESS OVER THE ABDOMEN.

MEN'S.   LADIES'.

SANITARY STOCKINGNETTE UNDER-VESTS,

PATENTED.

BENGER'S MAKE.

GUARANTEED PURE ANIMAL WOOL.

FOR MEN, WOMEN AND CHILDREN.

(When additional warmth is required.)

MEN'S.   LADIES'.

DOUBLE THICKNESS OVER THE CHEST.

Dr Gustav Jaeger, Professor of Zoology at Stuttgart University, introduced his 'Sanitary Woollen System' in the early 1880s. Based on the notion that 'being animals, we should wear animal clothing', he devised underwear made purely of wool, which, he claimed, was not only warm, but had the ability to 'repel noxious vapours'. His 'united garments' covered the entire body, and gained an ardent following, including both Oscar Wilde and George Bernard Shaw. But as the new century progressed, his underwear became less popular; his name has survived, but today, Jaeger is better known for top styles than for bottoms.

KNITWEAR

Few garments were created out of such a hard, working life as the most traditional knitwear. The original fisherman's sweater, as knitted by women right around the mainland ports, was known as a gansey. It was always navy blue, and the grease was left in the staple, for better protection against the cold, wet winds. The Scottish women were the most creative, knitting traditional patterns of ropes, diamonds and anchors into their garments; the patterns indicated a sailor's home port, both by the choice of design, and by the fact that where sailors had to carry boats down open beaches the shoulder ornamentation was heavier. It was said to be easier to recognise a drowned sailor by his gansey than by his face.

Technically, any fisherman's sweater knitted on the mainland is a gansey. The guernsey comes from the Channel Island itself, where Queen Elizabeth I established knitting guilds to supply the courts of England and France with knitwear. In recent years the two similar words have become confused, and even mainland garments have become known as Guernseys. But in fact, most fisherman's sweaters are not guernseys, but traditional ganseys. (The same mainland fishermen's wives also knitted traditional jerseys, which were not from Jersey; they were simply finer, thinner and more closely knitted garments, often made as gifts for a future husband.)

The first knitwear worn by gentlemen earned the term sweater because it was sold for that purpose, during the sporting explosion of the Victorian era. 'Open the pores!' ran one advertisement. 'Nothing will open them quite as well as a sweater.' At first they were made with the traditional round necks, then with v-necks edged with club colours. As mass production began, the modern distinction emerged between 'cut-and-sewn' knitwear, assembled from individual lengths of knitted fabric, and 'fully-fashioned', where the entire garment is knitted on a machine and is therefore more expensive. (The simple 'boat' neck was the result of a front and back 'cut-and-sewn' with a strip merely left unjoined.)

In 1868 the woollen waistcoat (with or without sleeves) was named after the Crimean hero, the Earl of Cardigan. This style was later popularised by Prime Minister Harold Macmillan as part of his comfortable, unflappable image, and by Rex Harrison as Professor Higgins in *My Fair Lady*.

Noël Coward admits that it was he who 'took to wearing coloured turtle-neck jerseys, actually more for comfort than effect, and soon I was informed by my evening paper that I had started a fashion'.

But despite these precedents, knitwear is still informal. This was confirmed by the launch of breakfast television in Britain,

Wool power – Knitwear will make even a suit and tie into an informal outfit. A cardigan, with its close relation to the style of the waistcoat, can best maintain formality, but as Michael Heseltine demonstrates, an ordinary sweater will make any outfit look more casual.

when it was decided to broadcast in a more casual and comfortable style. To change their image to suit, the presenters simply wore knitwear over their usual shirts and ties.

Necks

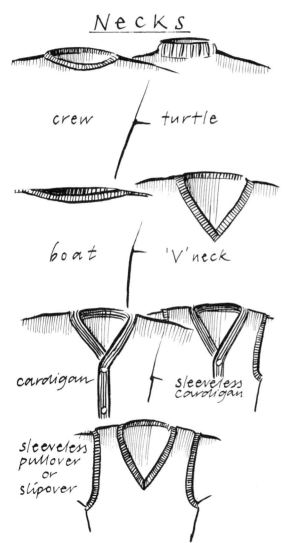

crew | turtle

boat | 'V'neck

cardigan | sleeveless cardigan

sleeveless pullover or slipover

Fine lambswool: suitable with suits

Cool cotton: the thing for spring

Midweight wool: the versatile style

Cable knit: with traditional twist

Rib knit: the straight and weighty

Aran knit: the fisherman's friend

ISLAND KNITWEAR

Legend traces the patterns on Fair Isle knitwear back to a bleak day in 1588 when *El Gran Griffón*, a ship of the Spanish Armada, was wrecked in the waters around the Shetland Islands. The Spanish sailors who were rescued from the vessel wore garments that bore Moorish designs, and using organic dyes from the wide range of plants and lichen growing on Fair Isle the islanders were able to copy the patterns into their knitting. And so, while Scandinavian influences can be seen in the knitting of the surrounding area, over 150 Fair Isle designs emerged, said to be based on the Armada Cross.

The 300,000 sheep dotted across the Shetland Islands are a unique breed, dating back to the Stone Age. Supported on a diet of rough pasture, heather and seaweed, they produce a uniquely soft wool which has been woven by the Islanders since the eighth century. To satisfy a demand for half a million garments a year, the weavers are now forced to mix wool from elsewhere into their clothing. But it is still possible, at a premium, to buy knitwear made solely of the soft, light and warm Shetland wool which Hillary and Tensing wore beneath their Everest equipment.

It was the Prince of Wales who made Fair Isle designs socially acceptable when, as Captain of the Royal and Ancient Golf Club, he teed off at St Andrew's in 1922 in one of their vivid patterns. 'I suppose the most showy of all my garments was the multicoloured Fair Isle sweater', he later wrote, 'with its jigsaw of patterns.' Subsequently it achieved a unique versatility, summed up by Peter York as being 'everything really ... it's period, it's provincial or posh'.

Sea chest – a fisherman in 1900,
clearly delighted with his
original, cable-knit gansey.

Shore thing – the traditional guernsey from Guernsey is at home today on land and sea.

Fair way – the Prince of Wales transformed the status of Fair Isle knitwear after he wore it on the golf course in 1922.

*N*IGHT ATTIRE

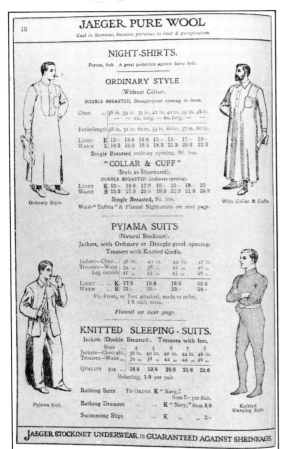

At one time gentlemen were offered three alternatives for sleeping. The traditional nightshirt, 'a great protection against damp beds', came in formal or informal versions – with or without collar. Expatriates had helped to introduce the idea of the new 'pyjama suits'. And there were also 'sleeping suits', which were knitted, and came with attached feet. All were made by Jaeger in pure wool, 'pervious to heat and perspiration' – there was no chance of a sheepless night.

Gentlemen's night attire has been gradually disappearing – along, one might suggest, with prudery, servants and badly heated bedrooms. In the wake of the nightcap, the nightshirt has become a rarity. Pyjamas are less and less common, and even the dressing gown is being replaced by dual-purpose bathrobes.

In fact the nightcap, the first item not to make it through the nights, survived a surprisingly long time, given that its real importance was in the seventeenth century when wigs were fashionable. Underneath their wigs men often had their heads shaved, so a nightcap was an essential accompaniment to a nightgown if a man was to be seen before he was properly dressed. And yet they survived long after this period; the Duke of Wellington clung stubbornly to his white wool, tasselled nightcap, which he wore during all his campaigns.

The word 'pyjamas' or 'pajamas', comes from the Urdu *pae jamah*, meaning leg garment, the loose fitting Persian pantaloons, tied at the waist, which are daytime wear in India and the Middle East. These first became night-time wear in England when they were brought back by returning colonials around 1880. But it was another fifty years before they replaced the nightshirt as the most common night attire. In the meantime, adherents of the nightshirt pointed out that their garment 'will not cut you in halves when you roll about the bed, or bisect you with a cord'. True, it might ride up; one whimsical suggestion was that men could reverse their sock suspenders and clip them to the hem of the shirt to keep it down. And nightshirts are still available today,

It Happened One Night – and the dress of
gentlemen on subsequent nights was altered
forever, when it appeared that Clark Gable slept
in pyjamas rather than a nightshirt.

although perhaps worn for effect rather than
for their effectiveness.

But the victory of pyjamas was acknow-
ledged in 1934, when Clark Gable wore them
to bed in *It Happened One Night* (the film
which also transformed men's ideas on
underwear). And in the privacy of men's bedrooms the garment worn by one of the era's
biggest sex symbols became the most vivid
in the wardrobe. Belisha pyjamas celebrated
the invention of the belisha beacon, with
black stripes on an orange background. And
throughout the 1930s novelty pyjamas appeared in colours so vivid that 'they threat-
ened to murder sleep'.

Pyjamas are still worn in combinations of
colours that would be inappropriate in any
male garments seen publicly, and cotton
pyjamas (brushed cotton in winter), with a
drawstring waist, have remained essentially
the same since the 1930s.

The dressing-gown began life as a long
robe which was worn informally indoors, and
in which, after the Restoration, gentlemen
could receive 'equals or inferiors'. But during
the Crimean war smoking became an acceptable and fashionable pursuit, and the
smoking jacket emerged, with its quilted
lapels, silk cords and oriental style. Gradually the two designs became intermingled, to
produce the silk dressing-gown of today.

It was Noël Coward who gave the silk dressing-gown its image of languid decadence. 'If
rumours and the illustrated weeklies are to
be believed,' said *The Sunday Times* in 1924,
'he writes his plays in a flowered dressing
gown and before breakfast.' The playboy
image still clings to the silk dressing-gown:

'Each morning sees
   some task begin,

Each evening sees
   it close;

Something attempted,
   something done

Has earned a night's repose.'

In 1924, Noël Coward achieved his first major success, acting in his own play, *The Vortex*. He took the role of Nicky Lancaster, a decadent son who spends a crucial part of the play in his night attire. 'With this success came many pleasurable trappings', wrote Coward, including 'An extravagant amount of pyjamas and dressing gowns, and a still more extravagant amount of publicity'. A combination of public association, dressing-room photographs and astute promotion by Coward himself soon linked him forever with his silk dressing-gown. It was, he wrote, 'temporarily good for business'. He claimed later to be irritated by the image but, over twenty years later, on his way back to London, he still stopped to buy dressing-gowns and pyjamas from Sulka in New York.

in fact, Hugh Hefner, publisher of *Playboy* itself, is traditionally photographed in one.

The alternative is the same style of gown although in a quieter cotton, or the 'woolly' dressing-gown, whose popularity also dates back to the 1920s. This was originally made out of cotton blanket, its trimming and twisted, tasselled cord made out of rayon, then a newly-created artificial imitation of silk. Its image of practical warmth continues to provide a staid alternative to the racier reputation of the silk gown. And the dressing-gown is perhaps the strongest survivor amongst the original range of night attire, in an age when a nightcap has become just a glass of Scotch.

The design of the woolly dressing-gown relates it directly to the smoking jacket, with its tasselled cords and decorated pockets. At the height of their popularity, materials ranged from plain wool, through camelhair and cashmere, to the luxury of vicuna.

SLIPPERS

Anatole France claimed that one of the privileges of his fame was that he could wear his slippers to the opera if he wished. Bob Geldof went further, and wore a pair of black velvet embroidered slippers, from Trickers in Jermyn Street, right across Ethiopia. That elegant style, bearing a monogram, crest or decoration in gold wire, is known as an Albert slipper; black leather, tapestry or the homely check wool uppers offer less sophisticated alternatives. The best slippers are made with padded interiors and light leather soles, and they are as loved and cherished by fathers as they are feared by their sons.

PART II

Accessories

'It has long been an axiom of mine
that the little things are infinitely
the most important.'

SHERLOCK HOLMES

*B*ELTS & BRACES

A 'brace' is designed to tighten a grip, and that is exactly what the first braces did; they tightened buckskin breeches, at the end of the eighteenth century, for a stylishly close fit. Labourers, who wore looser trousers, stuck to the original 'gallowses', which had appeared nearly a hundred years earlier, and from which their leggings simply 'hung'.

Those first 'gallowses' braces had an H-back; in the eighteenth century they crossed over in an X-back; and finally the forked Y-back, still retained on most formal braces, was introduced around 1850. And of course the original braces were made of materials like silk and satin, and fastened on to the trousers with buttons. They were also heavily patterned, often embroidered by a sweetheart. Debussy's braces were floral patterned; Napoleon's carried his personal bee insignia; and Queen Victoria gave Disraeli a pair sporting a fox-hunting pattern. Even Franklin D. Roosevelt had a pair bearing flags and eagles.

The hot summer of 1893 first drove City

Belt up – now, belts can go right around every style: they stretch from the elastic sport and schoolboy belt with S-buckle (top), through the canvas belt with leather buckle mount for casual wear, to the polished or patterned leather belts with brass buckles for suit trousers.

Brace yourself – left to right: traditional felt braces with elastic back; striped elastic braces for a sportier look; embroidered florals in the Victorian tradition; and modern, X-back elastic braces with clips, which will keep up trousers if not traditions.

gents 'to dispense with braces and wear sash or even belt ...'. Ironically, braces are actually cooler than belts, because they allow air to circulate more freely. But both the removal of jackets, and the emergence of the two-piece suit, both exposed braces to view, which was considered bad manners, and the belt began to gain acceptance in formal and business wear. At the start of this century few good trousers were made with belt loops; now, few are made without them.

To maintain formality, belts should be of leather, and always darker than the trousers. For casual wear they can be of a lighter colour, and made of elastic or of military webbing. But the height of elegance is still a pair of fine braces, with buckskin fittings with cat-gut ends and brass levers, the best possible way to keep up appearances.

Has tradition been suspended in the modern City? Not when the market looks for support.

JEWELLERY

'They say that gold is the heaviest of metals,' wrote Giordano Bruno, 'yet nothing else makes a man so agile, light-headed and capricious.' Those were exactly the characteristics that Victorian gentlemen wanted to suppress; and we still retain their notion that a serious man avoids all but the most discreet and functional jewellery.

The oldest is the signet ring, which was used to confirm identity before writing, and dates from pre-Roman times. The right to wear a signet ring was only granted to certain citizens or officers, and it marked out a man of property. Originally a gold band was simply hammered flat at one point to create the 'table' on which a seal was engraved. But this was limited in size; a larger table could only be created by casting. And so the characteristic head of the signet ring evolved, with the table flanked by 'shoulders' that may be stepped or engraved.

The true signet ring bore a seal, crest or other personal identification. But it is also used now to carry a single precious stone, 'gipsy set', where the stone is dropped into a recess, often star shaped, in the table.

Pins became widespread in the eighteenth century for securing cravats. Carved ivory and precious stones were popular; Napoleon favoured cameos, and those mourning the

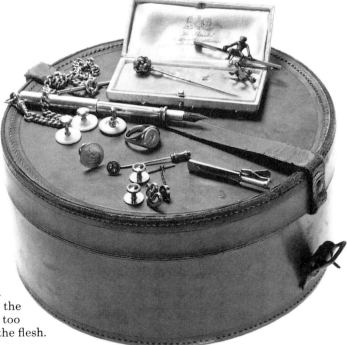

On your metal – As the cravat gave way to the tie, so stockpins (shown inlaid with stones, and in case) gave way to tie-clips (shaped as cricket bat); tiepins (with monkeys); and tietacks (shaped as coiled snake, with buttonhole anchor). Studs (brass and inlaid) are vanishing along with separate collars. But the signet ring (centre) survives, the only jewellery it's not too flash to wear against the flesh.

CUFFLINKS

Cufflinks first appeared in the nineteenth century because it was easier to link starched cuffs than to button them. The original cufflinks were chain-linked, and often made as imitations of buttons; subsequent years saw press-stud links (like the Kum-A-Part Kuff button of the 1930s) and expanding chain links, which lengthened under tension when the sleeves were pushed up, and were known as torpedo links. But despite modern innovations, like jointed barrel closures, the chain is still the way to maintain proper links with tradition.

Classic decorations still include imitation buttons, in gold and mother-of-pearl; these, like settings of precious stones, can be made up into complete dress sets of links and studs. Crests, enamelled designs, and engraved patterns or monograms are all ways of improving the wrist action, while an expensive extravagance are hand-paintings under crystal links. All in all, there is a wealth of ways to wear your art on your sleeve.

death of Queen Victoria wore jet (a form of black petrified wood) and pearl (the symbol of tears). Now, antique pins are being revived and worn in buttonholes. Modern pins designed for ties rather than cravats have a detachable back and chain, which anchors the tie to a buttonhole, and stops it blowing awry. (Tie-clips, which clamp ties to shirts, only look correct with narrow ties.)

Sadly, the elegant Edwardian matching dress studs and buttons (to say nothing of traditional collar studs) are rarely worn today, partly because there are few shirts which will take them. Other jewellery is largely looked down upon, particularly if worn next to the skin. In fact, the only things golden that a gentleman truly covets are silence and rules.

Watches

On 26 April 1968 the Swiss suspended their annual competition for accuracy between wristwatch chronometers. Measured against zero time error, a mechanical watch achieved astonishing accuracy, with an error of only 1.73. Yet after sixty years of endeavour to obtain that score, it was humbled by a quartz wristwatch, with an error of 0.152. The competition had become meaningless; it was never revived.

Once gentlemen looked down on watches. 'I never had a watch nor any other mode of keeping time in my possession,' declared Hazlitt, 'nor ever wish to learn how time goes.' It was considered rather vulgar for a gentleman to be concerned about the passing of time. But in Victorian society the gold hunter or half-hunter pocket-watch, a practical and therefore acceptable piece of jewellery, became the symbol of a successful member of the establishment. (A hunter has a solid metal cover over the dial, a half-hunter has the centre of the cover made of glass.)

It was only when the pocket-watch proved to be impractical in the trenches of the First World War that the wristwatch, previously a decorative toy for ladies, began to be worn by men. The first purpose-made wristwatch was designed in 1904 by Louis Cartier for his friend the Brazilian pilot Santos-Dumont, who wanted to read the time without removing his hands from the controls. Cartier still make a Santos watch today, but sadly it bears little relation to that first design. The Cartier Tank watch, however, still follows its original 1917 design, and has become a classic (and widely copied) watch.

Since then there have been many milestone wristwatches, which tell a story as well as the time. The Rolex Perpetual of 1930, the first really practical and long-lived self-winding watch; the Hamilton 500A of 1957, the first successful electric watch; and the Bulova Accutron, the tuning-fork watch of the 1960s which guaranteed an accuracy of two seconds a day.

But the quartz watch has destroyed forever the link between price, craftsmanship and function. The most accurate watch is not the product of years of accumulated skill; the most expensive watch cannot be justified in terms of function alone. The watch is unlike anything else in the Englishman's wardrobe – for here, the classic has been superseded.

'Do you think I could ever wear a watch?'
asked Pelham, Edward Bulwer-Lytton's fictional
dandy of the 1820s. 'I know nothing so plebian;
what can any one, but a man of business,
who had but nine hours for his counting-house
and one for his dinner, ever possibly want to know
the time for? An assignation, you will say.
True; but ... if a man is worth having
he is surely worth waiting for!'

The pocket watch, symbol of Victorian success, with the half-hunter (with half glass cover) shown below.

The revolutionary Bulova Accutron, which dragged the wristwatch through the quartz.

Sometimes reserved as an evening watch, the Tank has become the most widely imitated design in the world.

Cartier claim that the wristwatch first took flight with their design for the Brazilian aviator Santos-Dumont.

For the first time you could relax with Rolex and let your watch wind itself.

Handkerchiefs

Paisley patterns – silk for showing, cotton for blowing.

Well spotted – the best for the breast.

Hand-rolled edges – the winning linen.

Hemmed in – and monogrammed in style.

'What, he does not blow his nose by using his fingers?' demands a character in *Danton's Death*. 'He has a handkerchief? He is an aristocrat! Hang him on a lamp post!'

The use of a handkerchief has not always been a matter of life or death, but it has been a sign of gentility since the sixteenth century, when Erasmus wrote that 'To wipe your nose on your sleeve is boorish'. And it has changed surprisingly little over four centuries; the best handkerchiefs are still made of linen, which maintains its crisp, starched appearance, and the most expensive still have hand-rolled edges, because no machine can yet copy this finish successfully.

Lawn handkerchiefs were once also made of a linen material, from Laon in France, which gives them their name. Now lawn is a high quality, polished cotton, second only to linen itself.

Cotton handkerchiefs only became available from the middle of the seventeenth century, and they boomed in popularity with the craze for snuff. Printed handkerchiefs were acceptable to disguise the snuff stains, but then as now, and as with shirts, white remains the proper colour for gentlemen.

Only the paisley pattern has remained acceptable among coloured pocket handkerchiefs. This pattern is derived from Kashmir shawls, which first reached Western Europe around 1800, and were copied by the weavers in Paisley, Scotland. The curled figures of the paisley pattern are a symbol of unfolding life, known in India as *buta*, meaning flower, but known in Paisley as 'pines'.

Other coloured, spotted and silk handkerchiefs are now reserved for the breast pocket. (The paisley can also be worn in the breast pocket, but only in the puff fold, popularised by Fred Astaire.) The straight, TV fold of the 1950s has largely been replaced by the looser triangle and multi-pointed folds. Their formality can be increased by using plain, crisp linen handkerchiefs instead of coloured silk.

Handkerchief folds

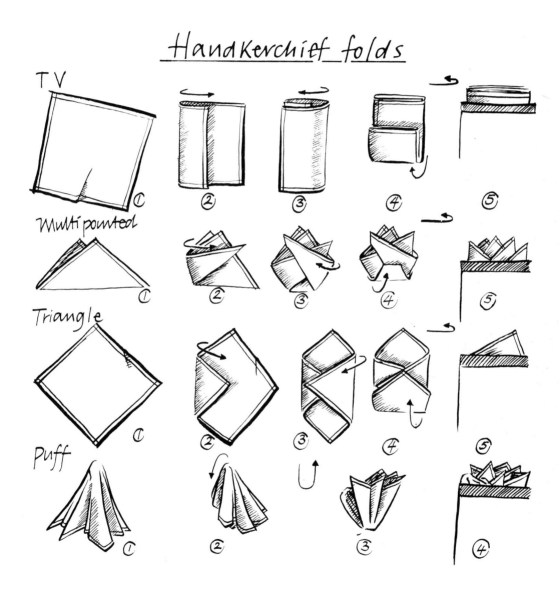

TV

Multi pointed

Triangle

Puff

Sticks & Canes

Voltaire had eighty of them, Rousseau forty. Napoleon had one made of tortoiseshell with a tiny musical box in the handle, where Henry VIII had an astronomical clock. And Benjamin Disraeli took two on his Grand Tour of 1830. 'I have also the fame', he wrote, 'of being the first who crossed the straits with two canes, a morning and an evening cane ... I changed my cane as the gun fired 6.'

A malacca cane is still an enviable possession. With a distinctive natural ridge along its length, it is sold as full, three-quarter or half malacca. The steps, the sections between the knots in the original length of cane, are rarely a 'full' stick's length

Sticking out – a fine stick was an essential accessory for the man about Regency town.

apart; for cheaper sticks either a quarter or half the length is planed down from a broader step to give the finished stick a uniform thickness. The planed sections rarely keep their looks as well as the unplaned bark.

Partridge cane from China, rattan (a class of palms with reedy smooth stems), and the 250 varieties of ebony, have provided some of the finest canes, topped with silver, jasper or the amber 'clouded' handles popular in the Regency period. They are still an elegant accompaniment to formal dress. But for everyday use, the wooden sticks originally used only in the country have gradually taken over in town as well.

Asked to make a stick from each suitable British wood alone, James Smith & Son produced seventy different types. Only one has remained exclusively for country sticks – the Irish Blackthorn, whose fine-grained bark stays on the stick throughout its life, and which comes from the tree under which St Patrick rested in the fourth century. Generally speaking, all other unpolished woods are suitable for country sticks, and all polished woods for town.

There are six basic styles of handle from which to choose. Three – the rondel or ball, the flat polygon and the ornate imago – are used for both walking-sticks and formal canes. And three are reserved for walking-sticks alone. The crutch is often a natural feature of the wood; the crop handle, popular in riding, is halfway between this and the classic crook handle. But the crook has dominated modern sticks in both town and country. And its acme has been defined, as being a handle 'as round as an early Norman arch'.

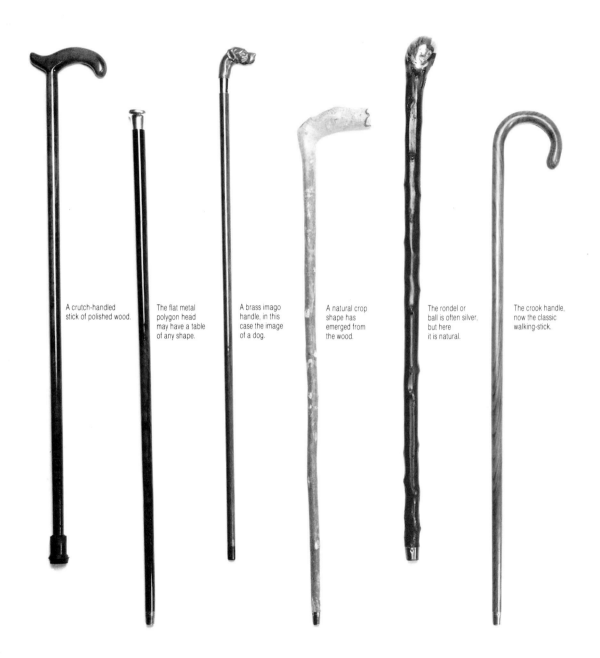

A crutch-handled stick of polished wood.

The flat metal polygon head may have a table of any shape.

A brass imago handle, in this case the image of a dog.

A natural crop shape has emerged from the wood.

The rondel or ball is often silver, but here it is natural.

The crook handle, now the classic walking-stick.

UMBRELLAS

'All men are equal,' wrote E. M. Forster. 'All men, that is, who possess umbrellas.'

Although popularly credited with the achievement, Jonas Hanway did not invent the umbrella; it can be found in ancient Greek and Roman art, and Hanway himself encountered it in Portugal. But he was responsible for introducing it to London in 1756. Unfortunately it had a mixed reception, laughed at by children, and abused by hansom cab drivers (who saw it as competition). Even the gentry were suspicious, since, as the Marquis of Carracioli observed, 'Those who do not wish to be taken as belonging to the vulgar herd, prefer to risk a wetting rather than be looked upon as pedestrians in the street, for an umbrella is a sure sign that one possesses no carriage.'

But Robert Louis Stevenson could see why the umbrella was gradually accepted. As opposed to carrying an ornamental cane, he felt '... the carriage of an umbrella came to indicate frugality, judicious regard for bodily welfare, scorn for mere outward adornment, and in one word, all those homely and solid virtues implied in the term Respectability'.

Early umbrellas had heavy oil- or wax-glazed linen covers, with ribs of Indian cane; these were superseded by silk and cotton covers on whalebone ribs. But umbrellas remained bulky, clumsy objects until Samuel Fox, a Derbyshire wire-drawer who made wire for crinolines, began production of U-section steel ribs in 1852. 'Nothing equal to

REACTION.

GENTLEMAN (to great Swell). "Why, Sid, what the douce makes you carry such a Thing as that!"
GREAT SWELL. "Aw, the fact is, you know, every Snob, you know, has a Little Umbrella now, you know; so I carway this to show I'm not a Snob, you know."

The Duke of Wellington was astonished when, during action at Bayonne on 10 December 1813, officers of the Guards put up umbrellas because it was raining. 'The Guards may in uniform, when on duty in St James's, carry them if they please,' he informed the colonel, 'but in the field it is not only ridiculous but unmilitary.' But it did please the Guards to carry them – and so the tightly furled umbrella became an historic part of the Guards' town and civilian uniform.

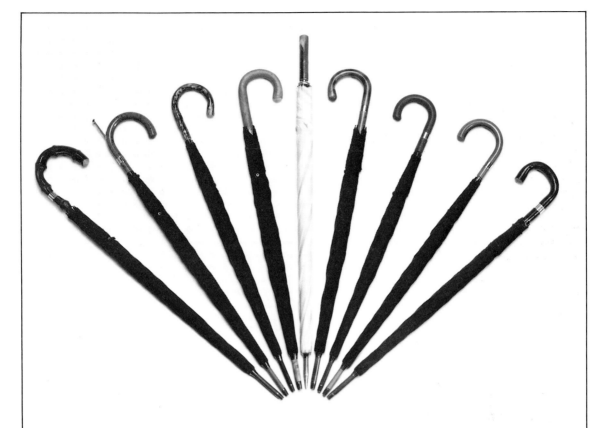

From whangee cane to leather covered through every shade of polished wood. Note the straight handle of the golf umbrella (which has a larger canopy), and the pencil hidden in the handle of the racing brolly.

To furl an umbrella properly, hold the handle in the right hand, and grip the ferrule in the left, with folds lying neatly, one over the other, on the left of the stick. The *bottom* fold should carry the fastener. Then turn the handle clockwise, at the same time bringing the left hand towards the handle, still gripping tightly. This will wind the folds neatly around the stick, leaving it ready to fasten.

it has ever yet been brought out,' he claimed. The Fox frame was patented in April that year, and in 1873 gained its patent curved ribs, which brought the tips closer to the handle and made the brolly even neater. Fox achieved a lasting reputation; and the umbrella achieved its elegant modern form.

In the City some gentlemen carry them unfurled, a habit which originated at Eton, where only the élite Pop pupils are allowed to roll their umbrellas. But in the country, 'unless he be a clergyman', it used to be considered 'unspeakably non-U' for a gentleman to carry an umbrella at all.

CASES

There are now many ways to carry off your business in style, but all of them derive from a limp satchel used in the fourteenth century for carrying money and valuables. It was called a 'budget', from which we get the financial term of today.

Originally document cases were made of Morocco, sheepskin or other light leathers, which required some kind of stiffening or backing, and a lining. Now, these have largely been replaced by cases of stronger unstiffened split-cowhide. (Split-hide is the top, grain portion of a hide which has been split through into two or more layers, to produce a leather of uniform thickness.)

Case study –
the capacious, metal-frame briefcase, descended from the Rosebery bag.

Bridle leather (a curried leather made from oxhides), casehide and the slightly thicker foliohide are firm leathers with a glossy finish; foliohide commonly has its flesh side 'mossed', which gives it a smooth, white surface inside the bag. This finish is usually found in metal-frame briefcases. Godillot of Paris first used a hinged iron frame on a carpet bag in 1826; from that came the Gladstone bag and the Rosebery, an oval-top bag from which derives the modern metal-frame briefcase (sometimes derisively nicknamed the 'lunch pail').

On limp cases a smooth leather would crease, and so a 'grained' leather is more suitable. Grained leather has its surface pattern brought out, rather than smoothed over. The grain disguises marks and creases, and also looks more natural; in a full-grain baghide or casehide the follicle pattern is clearly visible.

Lighter leathers, such as pigskin, calf and morocco, are usually reserved for underarm cases, like the portfolio (which gets its name from the Italian *portare*, to carry, and *foglio*, a sheet) and the folio case, which is a portfolio with a retractable handle. But fine leathers can also be stretched over the solid frame of the attaché case. This feature developed from the nineteenth-century portmanteau, a heavy, solid hide leather bag; to lighten its weight, a split-hide was stuck on to a stiff millboard foundation to make the first leather suitcase. Reduced in size, this became the traditional 'lid-over-body' attaché case. Modern cases are also 'box' style, with lid and body meeting; and millboard has been replaced by lightweight wood or steel, to bring the case history right up to date.

Open and shut – how the
case is framed.

Inside story – expanding
pockets inside the attaché
hold papers in place.

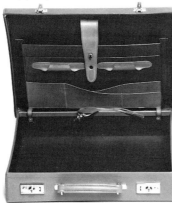

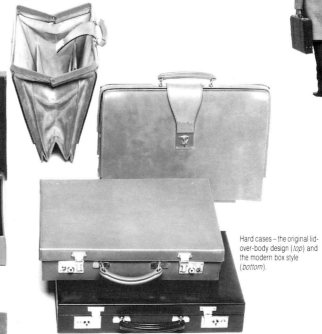

Hard cases – the original lid-
over-body design (*top*) and
the modern box style
(*bottom*).

No chances – locks and
straps for safety's sake.

Better battered – like its
owner, leather works long
and hard.

Do not handle – the
traditional *portafoglio* is
simply carried underarm.

Getting to grips – the folio
case adds retractable
handles to a portfolio design.

*W*ALLETS

The English monarch is not allowed to carry any cash at all; the best that a gentleman can do is to conceal the amount of cash he carries.

Wallets are made in two basic folded shapes: the square hip-pocket, and the oblong breast-pocket wallet. (There is also the unfolded oblong dress notecase, for carrying a little money without disturbing the line of a dinner jacket.) Particularly abroad, English men tend to carry either style in their breast pocket; as the seventeenth-century proverb has it, 'In the kingdom of a cheater, the wallet is carried before.'

There are two kinds of construction of small leather goods. 'Cut edge' items are made from thin but firm leather like cowhide or pigskin, stitched together so that the cut edges are visible, which are then given a polished or coloured finish. (This is the sort of finish usually found around the edges of leather keyrings.) The alternative, more widely used for wallets, is 'turned edge', where the leather is shaved down to a feather edge which is then turned over on to the opposite piece, stuck down and stitched. This is ideal for the thinner, softer leathers such as calfskin; a true calfskin comes from an animal not yet weaned (about six weeks old). Morocco, another popular wallet leather, is a hand-grained goat leather, originally produced by the Arabs of North Africa. And some of the most expensive wallets are made from ostrich, lizard and crocodile, only sold in England since 1882, but all supple, elegant and eminently noteworthy.

Skin deep – the beauty of an ostrich wallet (the follicles show where the feathers originally grew) and a lizard evening notecase.

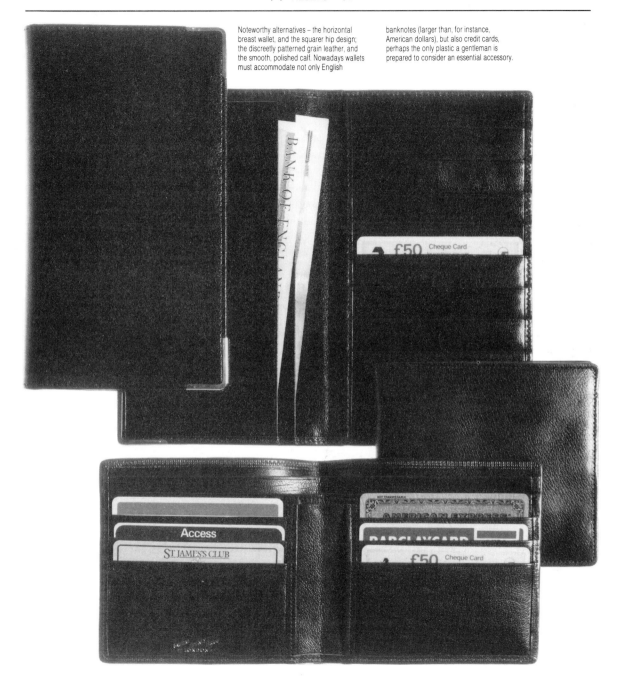

Noteworthy alternatives – the horizontal breast wallet, and the squarer hip design; the discreetly patterned grain leather, and the smooth, polished calf. Nowadays wallets must accommodate not only English banknotes (larger than, for instance, American dollars), but also credit cards, perhaps the only plastic a gentleman is prepared to consider an essential accessory.

SPECTACLES

Despite their supposed function, glasses have always been items of fashion. Once the fashion was for lorgnettes and quizzing glasses. In 1806 it was the monocle, 'worn with an air of conscious elegance'. In 1840, it was the pince-nez, and then, finally, the spectacles. But as late as 1900 the *Optical Journal* felt able to state that 'wearing spectacles out of doors is always a disfigurement, often an injury, seldom a necessity...'.

Today spectacles are designed to meet exacting optical standards. Traditional shapes, such as the half-moon reading glasses and the circular lenses of the first National Health spectacles, have survived, but traditional materials like tortoiseshell and horn have been superseded by plastics, and shapes and colours are ordered to suit the face of the wearer. The only modern classics in spectacle design are the perfectly round black frames designed by architect Le Corbusier.

But while styles in spectacles come and go, one design of sunglasses has reigned for fifty years. Coloured lenses had been available since the nineteenth century, but when aviators first rose above cloud level, they were dazzled by brilliant sunlight of a kind never experienced on the ground. The US Army Air Corps went to Bausch & Lomb, America's first optical glass company, for a solution, and in 1930 they came up with the aviator sunglasses, released to the public six years later, and known today as Ray-Bans. These glasses were precisely designed for use by military pilots. The 'teardrop' shape of the lens was arrived at by mapping the range of human peripheral vision; the green lenses have a light-absorption curve that resembles the colour sensitivity curve of the eye; and every lens is tested by dropping a steel ball on to its centre from a height of 50 in. These glasses leave all others in the shade.

Royal sun – Prince Andrew shows that smart pilots still wear the original aviator glasses, first designed for the US Army Air Corps. Initially called Anti-Glare Goggles, they were fortunately renamed a year later, and are still known today as Ray-Bans.

P. G. Wodehouse's *Rules for Novelists* (1930):

'(A) Spectacles: These may be worn by (1) good uncles, (2) clergymen, (3) good lawyers, (4) all elderly men who are kind to the heroine; by (5) bad uncles, (6) blackmailers, (7) money-lenders.

'(B) Pince-nez: These may be worn by good college professors, bank presidents and musicians. No bad man may wear pince-nez.

'(C) Monocle: This may be worn by (1) good dukes, (2) all Englishmen. No bad man may wear a monocle.

'(D) Those beastly tortoise-shell-rimmed things: Never worn in fiction.'

Round: rimmed

Round: covered wire

Library

Pince-nez
with ribbon

Half-moon

Round: gold-rimmed

Pince-nez

Monocle

GLOVES

'A gentleman is known by his gloves,' declared a nineteenth-century book of etiquette, and Count Alfred D'Orsay was known for wearing six pairs a day. After the reindeer gloves for his morning ride, the chamois for hunting and the beaver for the ride back to London, there were the braided kid gloves for the afternoon's shopping, the yellow dogskin for a dinner party, and then the lambskin embroidered with silk for the evening ball. It made each day into a five-finger exercise.

Even the average gentleman was expected until comparatively recently to have kid gloves for a ball. Light cotton or lawn gloves were required for summer social occasions. And for everyday use, 'the manly buckskin', or perhaps 'the elegant kid'.

The phrase 'fits like a glove' should be measured against Beau Brummel's gloves, which fitted him so that the outline of his fingernails could be seen. Fine gloves originally had eight components: a palm and back; a thumb; three 'fourchettes' or forks, which form the sides of the fingers; and three 'quirks', diamond-shaped pieces inserted at the bottom between the fingers. Nowadays, however, most gloves are simply a front and a back stitched together, with 'gores' between the fingers to give the necessary depth. Good gloves are still finished with three lines of pointing on the back, which first appeared in 1780, a vestige of the embroidery of earlier periods. But gloves have lost the significance they had when no gentleman would have sat in a church or theatre without wearing a pair. 'Some gentlemen insist on slipping off their gloves before shaking hands,' noted one guide on etiquette, going on to dismiss this as 'a piece of barbarity, of which no lady will be guilty'.

The arrival of knitted gloves in the late nineteenth century was 'to be lamented as a matter of taste'. They have never been fully accepted as formal or business wear. Nor have driving gloves, which should be left in one's car (or ideally, on one's driver).

Cold comfort – Arctic explorers, who have perhaps the greatest need to keep their hands warm, do not wear gloves but mittens. Sir Ranulph Fiennes, who traversed both Poles, explains that mittens are warmer because the fingers are in contact and so can transfer body heat from one to another.

Normal formal – in fine leather.

Hand knit – informal wool.

Grey day – suede for morning dress.

Fine lines – on unlined pigskin.

Hand signal – driving in gear.

White night – cotton for evening dress.

Tough cuff – the protective leather gauntlet.

SCARVES & CRAVATS

Legend traces the origin of the cravat back to 1660, when a regiment of mercenaries from Croatia, who had been fighting with the armies of Sweden in the Thirty Years War, visited Paris in a victory celebration. Louis XIV admired the way that they wore bands of material tied around their necks; and soon this 'croat' neckwear had been adopted by the French.

Yet centuries before, Roman soldiers serving in Germania and northern Gaul wore a wollen *focale*, wound around the neck, with the long ends hanging loose upon the chest, to protect them against the unaccustomed cold. Here, it seems, lies the origin of the woollen scarf, worn for warmth, as opposed to the silk, muslin or lace cravat, worn for decoration.

By the nineteenth century the cravat dominated men's fashion. Rules governed its shape, size, colour, fabric, and the last twists of the scores of possible knots. Only the ascot, an innovation late in the century, was tied in a simple end-over-end fashion, and was worn for morning walks and sports.

As stiff, tall collars gave way to the turndown, the cravat gave way to the tie and the complexity of knots was forgotten. Today most cravats are tied like ascots, and worn beneath open-necked shirts, a strange shift into informality for what was once the most formal of garments. Even with morning dress, most formal cravats are now tied in the simple, end-over-end manner.

Only the scarf, a basically outdoor garment, has retained its original function throughout. It still keeps out the cold, from the informality of college colours, through the practicality of wool and cashmere mufflers, to the formality of white silk (which should never be worn once the overcoat has been removed). And perhaps its survival is understandable – after all, it has had 2,000 years in which to be tied and tested.

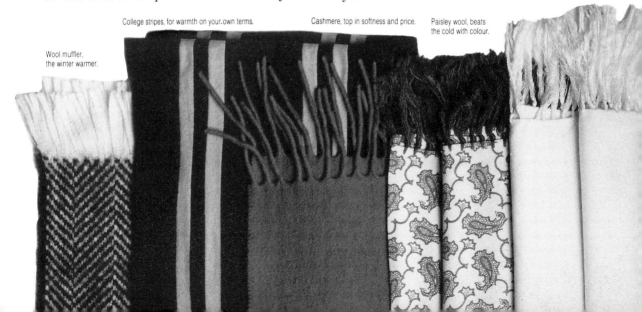

College stripes, for warmth on your.own terms.

Cashmere, top in softness and price.

Paisley wool, beats the cold with colour.

Wool muffler, the winter warmer.

THE RULE
OF THE CRAVAT

In 1828 H. Le Blanc published his definitive work, *The Art of Tying the Cravat*, which listed twenty-two different types of knot. It is still believed that the author was really Honoré de Balzac, who believed that the cravat was the only surviving true social indicator. Beau Brummell would leave a dressing room littered with crumpled cravats – 'Those, sir,' his valet explained to a visitor, 'are our failures' – and the way in which one tied and pinned a cravat was a clear indication of a man's self-esteem. M. Le Blanc agreed: 'The grossest insult that can be offered to a man *comme il faut*', he wrote, 'is to seize him by the cravat; in this place blood only can wash out the stain on either party.'

White silk, not warm but formal.

Formal stock, for morning formality.

Paisley silk, the boldest scarf.

Paisley cravat, now worn at weekends.

Spotted cravat, with pleated neckband.

*F*INISHING *T*OUCHES

There are some items which cannot be classed as clothes,
but without which a gentleman would not feel properly dressed.
Elasticated armbands, to lift cuffs above the wrist and away from toil;
a pen, the only essential tool for a gentleman's labours;
and a hip-flask and cigarette case, essential accessories
for a generation who believed that a drink before,
and a cigarette afterwards,
were the three best things in life.

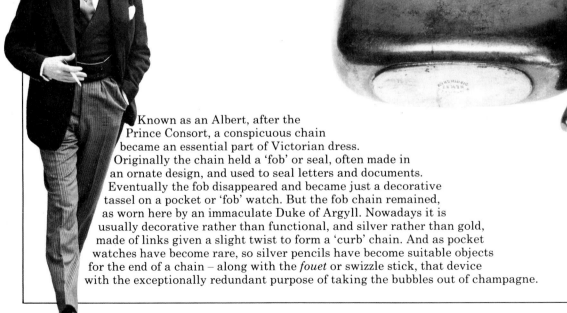

Known as an Albert, after the
Prince Consort, a conspicuous chain
became an essential part of Victorian dress.
Originally the chain held a 'fob' or seal, often made in
an ornate design, and used to seal letters and documents.
Eventually the fob disappeared and became just a decorative
tassel on a pocket or 'fob' watch. But the fob chain remained,
as worn here by an immaculate Duke of Argyll. Nowadays it is
usually decorative rather than functional, and silver rather than gold,
made of links given a slight twist to form a 'curb' chain. And as pocket
watches have become rare, so silver pencils have become suitable objects
for the end of a chain – along with the *fouet* or swizzle stick, that device
with the exceptionally redundant purpose of taking the bubbles out of champagne.

What should a gentleman wear in his buttonhole? A white or red carnation is the classic City *boutonnière*; the finest bespoke suits have a tiny loop behind the lapel to anchor the stem. Yet Joseph Chamberlain wore an orchid, and even stranger greenery has flowered from the buttonhole of Prince Charles, while Lord King favours a chain from buttonhole to breast pocket. But perhaps the ribbon of the *légion d'honneur* is the most impressive of all, and tailors will make their buttonholes a fraction nearer to the edge of the lapel to accommodate it more elegantly.

Summing Up

If, as the Bard suggested, the apparel oft proclaims the man, it's difficult to tell exactly what classic clothes reveal about a man's character. In 1840, Peter Buchan wrote indignantly, in *The Eglinton Tournament and Gentleman Unmasked*, that 'The title of Gentleman is now commonly given to all those that distinguish themselves from the common sort of people by a good suit of clothes. To the tailor and the barber alone, hundreds are indebted for the title of Gentleman.'

And only the year before, the author of *The Handbook of Swindling* declared that 'I have never yet known the instance of a swindler in a shabby coat. Read the Police Reports, how, nineteen times out of twenty, they commence "A young man, dressed in the highest style..." Hence a tailor is indispensable to the swindler.'

Originally only a true gentleman could understand and afford the niceties of classic clothes; then everyone came to enjoy their tradition and quality. But what cannot be picked up off the peg is the attitude to clothes and the *way* of wearing them which sets apart the landed and the merely loaded, the Sloane and his clone, and which puts that terrible English word 'class' into 'classic'.

It is almost impossible to lay down rigid sartorial rules, because they are immediately broken by the very figures who establish them. There was an old English expression that 'It is always Sunday afternoon on Cromwell Road' because the bourgeois of Belgravia strictly followed the rules of formal dress – while the gentlemen of Mayfair bent the very rules they had set up. The Duke of Windsor was a typical example of an immaculately dressed man whose innovations, such as brown suede shoes with a dark blue suit, were accepted, *because he knew better*. And, in fact, the well-dressed Englishman spurns the precisely matched outfit. 'My own audition apparel', recalled Noël Coward, 'was usually a navy blue suit with a coloured shirt, tie, socks and handkerchief to match. I had not learned then that an exact duplication of colours ill becomes the well-dressed man.' Later in life he learned his lesson, and repeated his view. 'It's hard, I know,' he wrote to Cecil Beaton. 'One would dearly love to indulge one's own taste. I myself dearly love a good match, yet I know

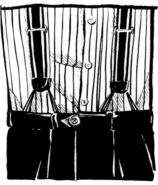

it's overdoing it to wear tie, socks and handkerchief of the same colour. I take ruthless stock of myself in the mirror before going out.'

The most wealthy and sophisticated English gentlemen often wear combinations of spotted ties and striped shirts, which would be condemned by the self-styled wardrobe engineers who set out to tell men how to dress for success. There is an English penchant for wearing an item of country dress, such as a Barbour, to the City, to demonstrate that one *has* a country house. And Fred Astaire's habit of throwing a new suit or hat against the wall would not have worn in clothes nearly enough to suit Lady Clare Rendlesham. 'The Duke of Devonshire is my pin-up man,' she told *The Times*. 'He has lovely frayed cuffs and collars, as if he had lent his new wardrobe to the gardener to wear in for six months. There's style for you.'

The English gentleman wears his classic clothes with a certain nonchalance, a studied indifference which can only be mastered by those who understand sartorial etiquette so well that they know just how and where to break with it.

If there are no rules, are there role models? Yes, but they bring problems of their own. Nicky Haslam, interior decorator to St James's Palace, wrote in *Vogue* that 'Not long ago I saw, crossing the Mall, that subtly well-dressed man, the Duke of Beaufort. That evening I went to drinks with a visiting American friend, having dressed as nearly identically as I could to the figure in the Mall: the perfect – I hoped – slope of the collar, the right size knot of tie, handkerchief casually overflowing from the breast pocket.

The *only* other person at the drinks party besides our beautiful hostess was the Duke of Beaufort.'

Trollope summed up the aim of every man who appreciates a classic wardrobe when he said that 'I hold that gentleman to be best-dressed whose dress no-one observes.' Sometimes there is an almost irresistible urge for the modern man to play the peacock, and to enjoy the ebb and flow of styles in modern menswear. But classic clothes retain their quiet, historic authority. They blend into the background because they are the correct, traditional clothes for a particular occasion; they merge with the dress of other senior figures because they have stayed the course of the century, to become the accepted dress of all gentlemen with authority, wealth and stature.

But classic clothes in themselves say nothing about class. Instead, they oft betray a certain discretion, a sense of correctness, and the quiet discipline required to stay on that highway of modern conservatism. In the face of seasonal fashions, designer labels and passing trends, it is with a combination of both restraint and relief that a man turns to utterly classic clothes. Nicky Haslam says, with almost palpable relief, that his frame is now firmly entrusted to Mr Johns at Savile Row tailors Johns & Pegg, 'whose taciturn approval provides the greatly needed self-respect; his tailoring naturally leads on to the quiet tie, the dark socks, the simplest shoe, the right shirt, that reeks, I hope, of class.

'But I cannot help thinking about that leopard-skin zoot suit in Johnson's down the King's Road. . . .'

PART III

The Complete Gentleman

'A man should look as if he had
bought his clothes with
intelligence, put them on with care,
and then forgotten all about them.'

HARDY AMIES

Morning dress

Now the most formal daywear in a man's wardrobe, the morning coat began the nineteenth century as a riding coat, since that was how a gentleman usually spent his mornings. Its curved front edges, which slope back at the sides, were designed to leave the rider's knees free from flapping coat fronts when in the stirrups. (Just as the two buttons on the rear of coats with tails are designed to fasten the tails up out of the way when riding.) Around 1906 the morning coat began to be fastened with just a single link button (a button on each end of a short chain) at the waist. At that time a gentleman was expected to have two other coats as well. The tailcoat, cut in across the waist, with a single- or double-breasted fastening, was originally worn throughout the day, but by the turn of the century it was reserved for the most formal evening wear. The frock coat, with tails and straight front edges, became the correct day wear, still worn by Prime Ministers and bank managers into the 1920s.

But as this century wore on, and the First World War transformed dress requirements, so the two coats designed for daywear began to battle for survival, both against each other, and against the lounge suit. Then in 1926 George v opened the Chelsea Flower Show in a black morning coat instead of a frock coat; gradually, the frock coat began to fade from society, until in 1936 Edward VIII abolished frock coats at Court, to replace them with the morning coat.

It was only in 1935 that grey became the predominant colour for morning dress at Royal Ascot. Morning dress for Court wear was black, with matching waistcoat and

Grey silk tie: pinned if possible. And even if visiting Windsor, the knot is four-in-hand.

Black morning coat (unless the rules say it's a grey day).

Top hat: better to hold on to tradition – don't try and wear it.

Waistcoat: the most formal is buff-coloured, the most popular is grey.

Striped trousers: the right lines.

Plain black Oxfords: polished to perfection.

striped trousers. Over the subsequent years, grey morning dress has become common – but black morning dress is the original and more formal of the two.

The Lord Chamberlain's office, which is responsible for Royal protocol, does not lay down a definition of morning dress. But then it has changed only in proportion to the amount it is worn – little. There has been a modern trend to wear a shirt with a stiff turndown collar and a formal, silver-grey silk tie known as a Macclesfield; according to the Lord Chamberlain's office, this is now 'usually taken to be the case' at Royal events. But it seems a shame, if one is wearing an outfit which is basically a century old, not to adopt as many of its original elements as possible. Which means a wing-collar shirt, and a black or grey ascot, 'asserted by a simple pin' as Eliot would say. Sadly though, it is no longer possible to get silk top hats. The only difference now lies between a 'pullover' – grey fur felt pulled over a gossamer frame – and the machine-made 'drab shell', which is becoming almost universal.

Beneath the coat should be a grey waistcoat, double-breasted if possible, and the original striped trousers. Matching gloves are another original accessory, together with a fine formal cane. And if they can be found, this is the only remaining outfit with which spats can still be worn. (Although, when the King opened the Chelsea Flower Show without them, the bushes were littered with the spats other gentlemen had discarded, and they never returned to favour.)

Today the opportunities on which a man can wear morning dress are likely to be among the most important in his life – prob-

Black and grey morning coats have been rivalling each other throughout the century. In 1935, grey became the predominant colour at Royal Ascot, and as that event remains the largest display of morning dress, grey has gradually become the more popular colour, particularly for other summer events. However, the traditions have not changed; black is still the proper colour for morning coats, paricularly at commemoration services. And even at weddings, one old rule of etiquette states that only the groom and viscounts are permitted to wear grey; all others must wear black.

ably his wedding, and possibly a Royal presentation. But 'morning dress is not regarded as obligatory at either Royal garden parties or investitures', and there is 'a fair sprinkling' of men who do not bother to wear it. Still, there will always be others who respect the history which it embodies, and perhaps like to have one outfit reserved for such special occasions. And the stewards at Ascot's Royal Enclosure will still turn away any guests who are not wearing full morning dress. While they do, its survival is ensured.

CASUAL DRESS

The sun, it was said, never set on the British Empire. And all the time it was beating down, English gentlemen maintained their strict formality in the face of foreign undress. Somehow, the same principle is still maintained when the sun comes out today.

The Englishman does not like taking off his jacket, because the shirt has always been regarded as an undergarment, and so improper for public display. In Fielding's novel *Tom Jones*, Mrs Deborah Wilkinson, 'tho' in the 52nd year of her age, vowed she had never beheld a man without his coat'. In 1912 a player was criticised for playing golf in shirtsleeves, which 'we have always regarded as against the etiquette of the game'. And even today a man cannot remove his jacket in the Steward's Enclosure at Henley.

The open-necked shirt has a respectable enough heritage – it was 'invented' by Byron, who hated the restriction of a cravat, and simply tore his off in frustration one day, letting his tall collar fall open. But it was difficult to wear separate, stiff collars unfastened, and so the fashion never really caught on, until attached collars became the norm relatively recently. And of course, there are still places today where a man will not be admitted or served without a tie.

So the English gentleman has found it hard to convert the formal shirt into a casual garment. He is still not entirely comfortable in a shirt without jacket or tie, and he does not like short-sleeved shirts (preferring to roll up the sleeves of an ordinary shirt when it is hot).

Only the invention by René Lacoste of the tennis shirt provided him with a

The polo shirt: short-sleeved, open-necked, and with a sporting pedigree, it almost forces a man to be casual.

Khaki chinos: originally made in Manchester, but it took the Chinese to get us cottoned on.

Argyle socks: the only diamonds a gentleman can wear with casual dress.

Boat shoes: Properly decked out, right down to the ground.

short-sleeved shirt he was prepared to wear in the summer without jacket or jumper – because it was a shirt which was actually *designed* to be casual, rather than a subversion of formality.

The gentleman has similar problems with his shoes. He has town shoes, country shoes and sports shoes, but little which is suitable for sun or sand. Foreign shoes like espadrilles are designed to be worn with bare feet, which makes an Englishman deeply unsure of his position, since to the English mind only a peasant or a pauper goes without hose. This leads to the cliché of the English traveller wearing socks under open-toed sandals.

The problem was solved when the boat shoe came over from America. This was invented by Connecticut yachtsman Paul Sperry when he noticed, on a winter morning in 1935, that his pet terrier was able to keep its footing on ice. A complex system of cracks under the dog's paw carried the water away and prevented hydroplaning. From this Sperry developed a herringbone pattern known as 'siping', and that became the sole basis of what is now the Authentic Original Sperry Topsider, a waxed leather boat shoe which can keep a man on his feet in appalling conditions. To the Englishman it is a tough, water-resistant and hence *practical* casual shoe, and it is conveniently associated with the seaside through a suitably serious (and expensive) sport. (And if he can't face wearing deck shoes on bare feet, colourful Argyle socks will look suitably casual.)

Khaki cotton trousers have an equally respectable place in the sun. They were created in 1848 by Sir Harry Lumsden, a regimental commander in India, who became irritated by the fact that the crisp white uniforms of his troops were immediately soiled by the dust. So he dyed the uniforms yellow-brown, using a mixture of coffee, curry powder and mulberry juice. And the locals dubbed the new uniforms *khaki* – the Hindu for 'dust-coloured'.

But whether their history is military or sporting, the English gentleman still feels slightly ill at ease in casual clothes. They lack the rigid rules of right and wrong that apply to other dress. With bright colours and bold patterns, they seem to lure him away from the sartorial straight and narrow. And he knows only too well that in England, as Cecil Beaton put it, 'Ridicule or scorn often reward those who turn off the modern highway of conservatism.'

'If a person turns to observe your dress,' said Beau Brummell, 'you are not well-dressed.' And after sunbathing became a fashionable pursuit in the late 1920s, a gentleman at the seaside was expected to wear little more than a tan. It was no longer enough to be *well*-dressed; one had to be *un*dressed. In Noël Coward's *Private Lives* Victor is revealed as an old bore by the way he insists that a suntan is 'somehow, well, unsuitable', while the fashionable Amanda wants to be 'done a nice crisp brown'. And soon it was the well-dressed gentleman that people turned to observe at the beach, the kind of man who claims that he won't sunbathe because he doesn't like to attract attention ...

COUNTRY DRESS

'A gentleman', declared Prince Albert, 'will borrow nothing from the fashions of the groom or gamekeeper.' So when country pastimes suddenly became popular, Victorian gentlemen had to find a warm, tough and functional outfit, which was clearly distinct from the working clothes of ordinary country folk. Their dress had to survive the rigours of the countryside, but declare that they were wealthy sportsmen rather than practical peasants. The result was the country dress which still sets the horseman apart from his groom today.

Once, London gentlemen looked down on country life. 'I nauseate walking; 'tis a country diversion,' moaned one of Congreve's fops. 'I loathe the country.' Then in the nineteenth century sports of all kinds became enormously popular, and the country in particular offered activities which were élitist, expensive, and often required large private estates. By Edwardian times gentlemen had become firmly attached to their hunting, shooting and fishing, and proud to wear an outfit which showed they were privileged enough to participate.

The essence of country dress is to blend in with the colours of the landscape in order not to frighten the game; the Victorians realised that vivid colours might 'cause the birds to turn, and the whole drive might be spoiled'. The writer Alison Lurie goes further, and points out that 'rural fabrics are usually soft and fuzzy. Tweed and wool and homespun repeat the textures of grass and bark and leaf, while corduroy, the traditional rural fabric, mimics not only the feel of moss but the look of a ploughed field'.

Cap: the peak of perfection. Flat, even when watching National Hunt.

Shirt: perhaps the only thing in Tattersall that every gentleman would buy.

Jacket: whether a Norfolk in Suffolk or a hacking in Hampshire, the only answer to the material question is tweed.

Trousers: corduroy, with 'the feel of moss and the look of a ploughed field'.

Shoes: like a country gentleman's character – solid, dependable, and polished without being flash.

The first gentleman's country outfit was a tweed suit, usually in a Cheviot tweed of moss green or brown. Knickerbockers with woollen socks were warm and practical; it is easier to wash a pair of socks than to clean

Apart from the occasional anachronistic golfer, it is only as part of country dress that knickerbockers have survived to the present day. The reasons combine practicality (it's easier to wash a pair of socks than to clean trouser bottoms), the timeless quality of the countryside (which seems to make notions of fashion rather irrelevant) and the toughness of tweed (which means that a pair of good knickerbockers will probably survive longer than father and possibly son as well). Prince Albert complained of his own son, Edward VII, that 'Even when out shooting he is more occupied with his trousers than with the game'; clearly he was worrying about wearing his father's knickerbockers instead.

trouser bottoms. The pleated Norfolk jacket, specially designed for shooting (see p. 38), introduced the idea that jackets could be of a different pattern from trousers, and by the 1920s it became a sign of wealth to have a separate jacket to be worn for sports. The most popular was a tailored tweed jacket, which was clearly distinct from a suit coat, yet versatile enough to be worn for other pursuits as well as shooting. Its natural colours made ideal camouflage, and tweed is both warm and strong; Edwardian butlers cleaned it by brushing with a special stiff brush with straw bristles, known as a 'dandy brush'. The most widely worn style now is the hacking jacket, which has angled flap pockets and still retains the three-button front common to all jackets in the 1920s.

The Viyella shirt, a mixture of wool and cotton, is similarly warm and comfortable; the classic country pattern is the Tattersall check (see p. 23). Either a towelling 'rain-choker' or stock is worn under an open collar, or a silk tie with sporting motifs adds the country equivalent of formality when necessary.

The outfit is completed with moss green or mustard corduroy trousers – which had, of course, a suitably regal origin, before they became working garments – and double brogues, with a welt between uppers and sole, heavier and stouter than their single brogue town equivalents. And in bad weather a Barbour is worn on top. Then a man is properly attired for the country – or, indeed, for Kensington at weekends, if, like Cowper's gentleman and so many men today, 'He likes the country, but in truth must own,/Most likes it when he studies it in town.'

TOWN DRESS

There are those who argue that the cut of the City suit is inextricably linked to the rise and fall of the financial indices. After the Wall Street Crash of 1929, for example, suits became darker, heavier, larger (the double-breasted suit came into fashion) and altogether more serious than the frivolous fashions of the 1920s. In the 1960s, when Englishmen had 'never had it so good', the waistcoat disappeared, buttons reduced from three to two, and the single-breasted style was *de rigueur*, producing a lighter, slimmer, less sober and straitlaced suit. But despite these changes in style, the basic rules of town dress have survived. Town dress is a clear indication of a man's position in life; his tie reflects his background, his suit reflects his income, and his shirt and shoes reflect his appreciation of both tradition and good taste.

The City clung to formal dress well into this century; the frock coat remained the proper dress for bank managers and brokers, and government brokers wore top hats to distinguish them on the trading floor. Now, the pinstripe suit, the uniform of the City, echoes the traditional striped trousers of formal dress.

'A proper function of the business suit', declared one tailor, 'is to offer a man a decent privacy, so that irrelevant reactions are not called into play to prejudice what should be purely business transactions.' Hence the popularity of the pinstripe suit (see p. 33), which has become so widely worn that it attracts no attention whatsoever in business circles. What *does* attract interest, however, is the quality of material and cut, and the detail of the tailoring; whether lines

Shirt: If not white then striped for action.

Tie: old school shows where you took those first serious steps.

Suit: no one suits themselves in the City; they follow the straight and narrow – pinstripe.

Trousers: the sharpest thing about a classic suit should be the trouser crease.

Shoes: if you mean business, shoes are always darker than the suit. That means black in practice, legal or otherwise.

continue unbroken over pocket flaps and shoulders, and whether cuff buttons can be undone. These reveal how much a man has been able to spend on his suit. (There was a story circulating which claimed that City men were ordering their suits with one cuff button for each £10,000 of their salary. In a City where salaries have reached £100,000 and more, this seems hard to believe.)

If the suit displays a man's present position, the tie displays his past. The most potent ties are still those of the top public schools; Oxbridge college (never university) and regimental ties are next in ranking. The gentlemen's clubs rarely have ties, since they are small enough for members to know each other. (A member of a Pall Mall club once asked in the suggestion book if they might have a tie like other clubs. The secretary replied, 'What *other* clubs?')

The Old Etonian tie still carries more weight than most, although in the newly meritocratic City that weight may either provide clout or prove a burden. An Old Etonian may also continue the habit of signalling his status by carrying his umbrella unfurled (traditionally at Eton only the self-electing élite group called Pop are allowed to furl their brollies; see p. 87).

As for shirts, the 'Bengal stripe' in dark red and white is now accepted in the City, but the classic town shirt still has the white collar which puts its wearer firmly among the 'white-collar' workers. Traditionally, that collar is a formal turndown or cutaway, and the shirt is *always* long sleeved; in City offices where jackets are removed, sleeves may be rolled up in hot weather, but short sleeves are never worn.

Finally, the rule with business shoes is that they must always be darker than the suit. In practice, this means black, and although moccasins are sneaking into some boardrooms, classic lace-up styles are still preferred.

'Man goeth forth to his work, and to his labour, until the evening'; and in Victorian business, professional men were expected to go forth in formal dress. Businessmen set out for work each day in a morning coat, poised as it was between 'the dressiness of the Frock' and 'the popularity of the Lounge'. Here, at the turn of the century, the morning coat is worn for work with the correct striped trousers, black top hat, and spats – plus the more familiar City accessories of umbrella, metal framed case and newspaper.

EVENING DRESS

The idea of wearing black for evening wear was first introduced by the nineteenth-century writer Edward Bulwer-Lytton, as a romantic gesture to suggest that he was 'a blighted being'. He gave further impetus to his own idea by writing, in 1828, that 'people must be very distinguished to look well in black'. It was a statement certain to challenge London's dandies.

The dinner jacket made its début in the United States in 1896, when Griswold Lorillard, a celebrated dandy, wore it to a white-tie-and-tails ball at an exclusive country club – in Tuxedo Park, New York. Hence the American term 'tuxedo' to describe the modern dinner jacket.

But for years, white tie (with starched wing-collar shirt and tailcoat) remained the formal dress demanded by English society. It was thanks to Edward VII, when he was Prince of Wales, that the dinner jacket transformed gentlemen's evening dress. The original, single-breasted dinner jacket was basically a tailcoat without a tail, complete with peaked lapels. It was first worn by the Prince of Wales for dinner aboard his yacht at Cowes, and then later at other semi-formal gatherings away from London. At first it was worn with the white pique waistcoat of formal white tie, but later with a black vest matching the fabric of the jacket and trousers.

The first double-breasted dinner jacket was reputedly ordered from Savile Row by song-and-dance man Jack Buchanan, and was popularised by the Prince of Wales in the 1930s. It remains the most acceptable alternative to the single-breasted jacket with peaked lapels, the classic design which

Bow-tie: Silk or barathea, properly tied. (If a gentleman can't tie it himself he trusts a valet, not a manufacturer.)

Dress shirt: Pleated front with French (turned back) cuffs and links. Never ruffles, and remember it's *always* all white on the night.

Dinner jacket: Single-breasted with peaked lapels. Shawl collars and double-breasteds are acceptable; notched lapels are more nightmare than evening wear.

Cummerband: If worn instead of a waistcoat, the pleats should always point up, or the effect is simply waisted.

Colour: Your greens, plums and burgundy belong on the table, not on your back. Black tie means just that – black.

Trousers: The trim on the seam is a relic of the braid on officers' uniforms. Don't mess with tradition.

Pumps: Bowed down to the ground, the traditional way to step out for an evening. Low cut and high style.

displays its derivation from the original tailcoat. The shawl collar model has a more subtle look, although it does accentuate a portly frame. But the jackets with notched lapels, which are the same as those on day-time jackets, are nothing but an effort by modern manufacturers to profit by using standard day-time jacket forms, and simply facing them in satin.

The ultimate colour for a dinner jacket is actually not black, but midnight blue. When the Duke of Windsor ordered a new dinner jacket in the 1920s, he specifically requested that the material should not be black, which takes on a greenish hue in artificial light. According to the Duke, under those conditions, midnight blue appears 'blacker than black'.

The Duke of Windsor completed the development of modern evening dress by ordering from his shirtmaker a soft, pleated-front formal shirt with double French cuffs and a turned-down collar, in place of the stiff, wing-collared shirt worn with white tie. So the quite literally rigid formality of the old white tie was broken down – but with a clear distinction remaining between day wear and evening dress.

The pleated front on a dress shirt should never reach below the waist, or it will buckle when the wearer is seated. Instead, the waist should be covered with a cummerbund, a sash originally worn in India (from the Hindu *kamarband*) and brought back by the British. The folds should always point up, because traditionally there was a small pocket between the pleats to hold opera or theatre tickets.

Dating directly to the sixteenth century,

The tail end of the transformation from white tie to black. The introduction of the 'dress lounge', later called the dinner jacket, heralded the modern style; the cummerbund replaced the waistcoat when officers brought it back from India, and the starched shirt later disappeared with the Duke of Windsor. But contemporary black tie should have peaked or shawl lapelled jackets, matching trousers and pumps of a century ago, all in darkest black. It's as true now as then that a gentleman 'attired for the gayest evening party, could, apart from his jewellery, be equally presentable at the most sorrowful funeral'.

pumps with bows are the oldest part of traditional evening dress. .Their name is believed to derive from the word 'pomp', because of their elegance, and although originally worn with knee breeches and silk stockings, they retain their style beneath modern trousers, and complete the traditional style of full evening dress.

Useful Addresses

This is a brief selection of some of the most intriguing purveyors of classic men's clothing. It is by no means comprehensive – it simply crosses a few of the more famous, worthwhile or simply traditional thresholds.

Tailors

Savile Row is an area rather than a street, and although the tailors guard the title jealously, Savile Row tailoring can also be found in the neighbouring Dover Street, Cork Street and Sackville Street (where some people say you can get the best . . .)

ANDERSON & SHEPPARD
30 Savile Row, London W1
Renowned for achieving elegance through softness rather than severity of line, their famous clients have included prime movers like Fred Astaire and Diaghilev.

HAWES & CURTIS
2 Burlington Gardens, London W1
Tailors to the Duke of Edinburgh, Prince Andrew and Prince Edward, and celebrated for their cloth as well as their cutting.

DOUG HAYWARD
95 Mount Street, London W1
Combines traditional skills with a modern approach to customer service and a relaxed atmosphere. Big with 'Sixties men who are now power potentates.

H. HUNTSMAN & SONS
11 Savile Row, London W1
Possibly the most famous, and probably the most expensive, bespoke tailors in England. They also boast a wooden horse in the fitting rooms, so you can check the fit of your riding gear.

DIMI MAJOR
11 Royal Parade, Dawes Road, London SW6
Magazine editor Peter Crookston was in a restaurant once when an American film producer was introduced to him for the first time. The producer looked him over as they shook hands. 'That's a nice suit Dimi made you,' said the producer. Peter has been a regular ever since, along with customers like Sean Connery, Paul McCartney and the Duke of Norfolk.

HENRY POOLE & CO.
15 Savile Row, London W1
The oldest of all the Savile Row tailors, their first appointment was to Emperor Napoleon III, and they have since furnished the wardrobes of half the world's royalty.

Shirts

Jermyn Street remains the centre of shirt-making, whether bespoke or off-the-shelf, and the range of colours, cottons and cuts you can get along this historic street remains unrivalled.

HARVIE & HUDSON
77 Jermyn St, London SW1
One of the most famous bespoke shirtmakers in England, they also make off-the-shelf sizes in the finest quality cotton and silk.

HILDITCH & KEY
37 & 73 Jermyn St, London SW1
Twice a year there are sales at H & K which have queues of customers out on the pavement for reduced prices on workroom shirts.

T. M. LEWIN & SONS
106 Jermyn St, London SW1
Top quality shirts, but at a notch below other Jermyn St prices, and in a complete range of collars – including tab and buttondown. Plus good range of school ties and bow-ties, and blazer buttons.

NEW & LINGWOOD
53 Jermyn St, London SW1
118 High St, Eton
New & Lingwood catch their gentlemen young, as they pick up good dressing habits while still at school, and then

continue the tradition in London.

THOMAS PINK
2 Donovan Ct, Drayton Gdns,
London SW10
16 Cullum St, London EC3
The new breed of young City slickers get their French-cuff shirts from Pinks at sub-Jermyn St prices, either at home in Fulham or at work in the City.

TURNBULL & ASSER
71 Jermyn St, London SW1
The most famous shirtmakers in the world with a vast range of material and a vast history of expertise. Bespoke or off-the-shelf, plus stunning array of ties.

Outfitters

CORDINGS
19 Piccadilly, London W1
All the classic country togs, from weatherproofs to wellingtons.

DUNN & CO.
Branches throughout Britain. One of the most traditional chains of outfitters, they always have a good range of Harris tweed jackets.

GIEVES & HAWKES
1 Savile Row, London W1
Famous for their uniforms, they made Prince Andrew's wedding outfit, as well as Bob Geldof's

morning dress. Off-the-peg suits, plus all accoutrements for City dressing.

HACKETT
65c New King's Rd, London SW6
(Plus branches)
With devoted attention to detail, Hackett not only sell refurbished original gentlemen's clothes, but now make their own new garments to the original specifications. Everything from suits and jackets, formal dress, superb tweeds and classic shoes down to the smallest accessories.

S. FISHER
22 & 32 Burlington Arcade,
London W1
12 The Market, Covent Garden,
London WC2
The Arcade branches specialise in the finest cashmere, wool, and beautiful hand-embroidered silk waistcoats. In Covent Garden there's a more country feel, with a huge range of Barbours, cords, Shetlands and Fair Isles.

Ties

T. M. LEWIN & SONS
(see Shirts)
One of the best selections of school and regimental colours in both ties and bow-ties.

SCOTT
57 Burlington Arcade,
London W1

Good range of official colours in ties and scarves, with all recognised colours available on order.

CASTELL & SON
13 Broad St, Oxford
This is where the undergraduates pick up college ties, scarves, blazers, and also crested links and buttons.

RYDER & AMIES
22 King's Parade, Cambridge
The Light Blue location for college and club ties, scarves, cravats etc.

Shoes

JOHN LOBB
9 St James's St, London SW1
The most revered bespoke shoemakers in the world. The first pair can take four months to make; then the hand-carved last is stored in their basement among the most famous feet in history. Fiercely expensive.

ALAN MCAFEE
5 Cork St, London W1
100 New Bond St, London W1
73 Knightsbridge, London SW1
46 Curzon St, London W1
The full range of classic English shoes, traditionally made and well constructed.

HENRY MAXWELL
11 Savile Row, London W1
Tucked into the basement of Huntsman's, and best known for their riding boots.

TRICKER'S
67 Jermyn St, London SW1
Their white-aproned assistants
serve up a selection from the
finest heavy, country brogues to
elegant embroidered slippers.

WILDSMITH & CO.
15 Princes Arcade, Jermyn St,
London SW1
Justly renowned for their light
and elegant penny and
tasselled loafers.

Hats

BATES
21a Jermyn St, London SW1
From country hats and caps in
every conceivable tweed to
formal trilbies and boaters, plus
their witty window displays.

HERBERT JOHNSON
13 Old Burlington St, London
W1
In the heart of Savile Row
territory, every design for town
and country from topper to
trilby.

LOCK'S
6 St James's St, London SW1
The hatters who invented the
Coke (or bowler to lesser
manufacturers), and are still
going strong in every
department.

Knitwear

Burlington Arcade is still a
centre for the best quality
knitwear, selling both
traditional working patterns
and the most delicate cashmere
from their elegant, wooden-
fronted shops.

W. BILL
93 New Bond St, London W1
Increasingly surrounded by
fashionable boutiques, W. Bill
staunchly maintains a tradition
of Shetlands, Fair Isles, Arans,
lambswools and cashmeres.

S. FISHER
(see Outfitters)
A fine selection of Arans,
Guernseys, Fair Isle and
cashmere knitwear.

WESTAWAY & WESTAWAY
65 Great Russell St, London WC1
92 Great Russell St, London WC1
The crofters organisations send
knitwear from the islands
direct to their shop, opposite
the British Museum. Lower
prices and a better selection
than anywhere else.

Leather

ASPREY
165 New Bond St, London W1
After the doorman has guided
you through the elegant curved,
sliding doors, avoid the gem-
encrusted statuettes and head
for the leather department, for
elegant wallets, notecases and
other goods.

SWAINE, ADENEY,
BRIGG & SONS
185 Piccadilly, London W1
Briefcases, portfolios, attaché
cases and the most elegant
wallets confirm the reputation
they have built up with ten
monarchs since 1750. They also
stock a wide range of
accessories, and the
incomparable range of Brigg
umbrellas.

Jewellery

There are now an increasing
number of outlets selling men's
original antique jewellery,
where you can pick up
beautiful examples of links,
studs and rings that really have
withstood the test of time. Try
... Or one of the few shops
which combine the best of old
and new:

PAUL LONGMIRE
12 Bury St, London SW1
A stunning collection of
antique cufflinks and pins,
together with ranges of
monogrammed, enamelled and
painted links which are made to
customers' own designs. Paul
Longmire's personal interest
maintains this as a unique
gentlemen's jewellers.

Sticks, Canes & Umbrellas

T. FOX
118 London Wall, London EC2
The home of the true City

umbrella – no gentleman in the Square Mile has any business going anywhere else.

SWAINE, ADENEY, BRIGG & SONS
(see Leather)

JAMES SMITH & SON
53 New Oxford St, London wc1
One of the few remaining traditional shops selling a spectacular array of sticks, umbrellas, shooting sticks, etc.

Americana

J. SIMONS
2 Russell St, London wc2
Importers of a wide range of American clothing, including cotton chinos, good quality US-cut jackets, and Bass Weejuns.

AMERICAN CLASSICS
404 King's Rd, London sw10
20 Endell St, London wc2
Carry a range of secondhand and new American casual wear, including well-worn Levi 501s, T-shirts and polo shirts.

BROOKS BROTHERS
346 Madison Avenue, New York
Founded in 1818, they make the most famous shirt in the world, and carry its tradition and quality through their entire range of menswear.

Dedicated to Sally,
who suits me best of all

ACKNOWLEDGEMENTS

With particular thanks to Geoff Goode Photographics for all the studio photography, and to the designer Harry Green without whom the book could not have been made to measure.

The author and publishers would like to thank the following for their help in supplying illustrations and for granting permission to reproduce them:
The Associated Press Ltd: p. 59
J. Barbour & Sons Ltd (Morris Nicholson Cartwright Ltd): p. 49
BBC Hulton Picture Library: pp. 29, 37, 69 (left),105
Burberry's Ltd: p. 50
Camera Press: pp. 23, 72 (left)
City of Westminster Libraries Archives Section/Jaeger (Photo: Godfrey New Photographics): pp. 65, 70, 72 (right)
Columbia Pictures Industries Inc (National Film Archive, London): p. 71 (above)
The Daily Telegraph: p. 22
Mary Evans Picture Library: pp. 111, 113
C. B. Ferry: p. 77
Keystone Press Agency: p. 14
London Management (Langton Gallery Ltd): p. 107
Levi Strauss: p. 56
Magdalene College Cambridge: p. 28
Men's Wear (Bath Museum of Costume Research Centre): p. 33
Museum of Eton Life, Eton College: p. 34
National Film Archive, London: p. 51
Kathy Nicholls: line-drawings pp. 10, 14, 15, 16, 19, 21, 30, 54, 67, 74, 83, 100, 102
Popperfoto: p. 64

Providence Journal Co.: p. 92
Punch Publications Ltd: pp. 52, 86 (left)
Rex Features: p. 24
Scott Polar Research Institute: p. 94
Scottish Fisheries Museum: p. 68
Sotheby's London: p. 15
Richard Swainson: pp. 47 (left and right), 55, 88, 89
Syndication International: pp. 36 (left), 40, 42 (left), 43 (right), 46 (right), 48, 62, 98, 99, 109
The Telegraph Sunday Magazine (Photo: Chris Holland): p. 39
Topham Picture Library: pp. 42 (right), 43 (left), 66, 86 (right)

The author and publishers are also grateful to the following who lent material for studio photography:
Austin Reed
Cartier Ltd
J. Dege & Sons Ltd
Gallery of London Ltd
Gucci Limited
Hunt & Winterbotham/Illingworth, Morris Plc
W. Johnson & Sons
Thomas Kettle Ltd
Paul Longmire Ltd
Swaine, Adeney, Brigg & Sons Ltd
Tricker's

Special thanks are also due to Jeremy Hackett and Ashley Lloyd-Jennings of Hackett Clothiers for their invaluable help and advice in both reading the text and supplying the majority of the items for studio photography.

Published in the United States in 1988 by Harmony Books,
a division of Crown Publishers, Inc.,
225 Park Avenue South, New York, New York 10003

Originally published in Great Britain in 1987
by George Weidenfeld & Nicolson Limited

HARMONY and colophon are trademarks of Crown Publishers, Inc.

Manufactured in Great Britain

Design by Harry Green

Library of Congress Cataloging-in-Publication Data
Keers, Paul.
   A gentleman's wardrobe.
   1. Men's clothing.   2. Grooming for men.   I. Title.
TT618.K44 1988   646′.32   87-21119
ISBN 0–517–56758–X
10 9 8 7 6 5 4 3 2 1
First American Edition